# DK EYEWITNESS WORKBOOKS
# Weather

by Nichola Barber

**Educational Consultants** Linda B. Gambrell
and Geraldine Taylor

**Senior Editors** Susan Reuben, Fleur Star
**Assistant Editor** Lisa Stock
**Editor** Avanika
**US Editor** Jennette ElNaggar
**Art Editors** Peter Laws, Simon Murrell, Tanisha Mandal
**DK Picture Library** Claire Bowers, Lucy Claxton,
Rose Horridge, Myriam Megharbi, Romaine Werblow
**Managing Editors** Christine Stroyan, Shikha Kulkarni
**Managing Art Editors** Anna Hall, Govind Mittal
**DTP Designer** Anita Yadav, Pawan Kumar
**Production Editor** Tom Morse
**Production Controller** Nancy-Jane Maun
**Senior Jacket Designer** Suhita Dharamjit
**Jacket Design Development Manager** Sophia MTT
**Publisher** Andrew Macintyre
**Art Director** Karen Self
**Publishing Director** Jonathan Metcalf

This American Edition, 2020
First American Edition, 2008
Published in the United States by DK Publishing
1450 Broadway, Suite 801, New York, NY 10018

Copyright © 2008, 2020 Dorling Kindersley Limited
DK, a Division of Penguin Random House LLC
20 21 22 23 24 10 9 8 7 6 5 4 3 2 1
001–323006–June/2020

A catalog record for this book
is available from the Library of Congress.
ISBN 978-0-7440-3457-8

DK books are available at special discounts when purchased in bulk
for sales promotions, premiums, fund-raising, or educational use.
For details, contact: DK Publishing Special Markets,
1450 Broadway, Suite 801, New York, NY 10018
SpecialSales@dk.com

Printed and bound in Canada

For the curious

www.dk.com

# Contents

## Fast Facts

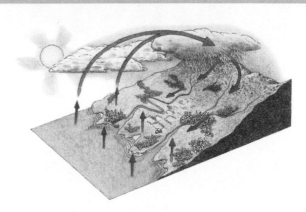

## Activities

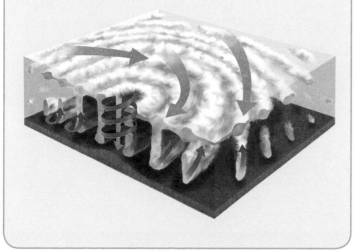

## Quick Quiz

# How This Book Can Help Your Child

**Eyewitness Workbooks** offer a fun and colorful range of stimulating titles in the subjects of history, science, and geography. Devised and written with the expert advice of educational consultants, each workbook aims to:

- develop a child's knowledge of a popular topic
- provide practice of key skills and reinforce classroom learning
- nurture a child's special interest in a subject.

## About this book

**Eyewitness Workbooks Weather** is an activity-packed exploration of the weather and how it affects our world. Inside you will find:

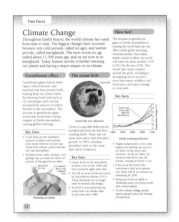

## Fast Facts

This section presents key information as concise facts, which are easy to digest, learn, and remember. Encourage your child to start by reading through the valuable information in the Fast Facts section and studying the statistics charts at the back of the book before trying out the activities.

## Activities

The enjoyable, fill-in activities are designed to develop information recall and help your child practice cross-referencing skills. Each activity can be completed using information provided on the page, in the Fast Facts section, or on the charts at the back of the book.

## Quick Quiz

There are six pages of multiple-choice questions to test your child's newfound knowledge of the subject. Children should try answering the quiz questions only once all of the activity section has been completed.

## Important information

Please ensure that your child does not look or point his or her camera directly at the sun in the cloud watching activity on page 22. All other activities in this book can be carried out without adult supervision.

# PROGRESS CHART

Chart your progress as you work through the activity and quiz pages in this book. First check your answers, then color in a star in the correct box below.

| Page | Topic | Star | Page | Topic | Star | Page | Topic | Star |
|------|-------|------|------|-------|------|------|-------|------|
| 14 | The World's Climates | ☆ | 24 | Stormy Times | ☆ | 34 | Weather Power | ☆ |
| 15 | The World's Climates | ☆ | 25 | Thunder and Lightning | ☆ | 35 | Pollution and Weather | ☆ |
| 16 | Light From the Sun | ☆ | 26 | Hail and Snow | ☆ | 36 | The Environment | ☆ |
| 17 | Ocean Currents | ☆ | 27 | Fog and Frost | ☆ | 37 | The Environment | ☆ |
| 18 | A Windy Day | ☆ | 28 | Mountain Weather | ☆ | 38 | Weather in the Atmosphere | ☆ |
| 19 | A Windy Day | ☆ | 29 | Land and Sea | ☆ | 39 | Sun and Earth | ☆ |
| 20 | Warm and Cold | ☆ | 30 | Weathering and Erosion | ☆ | 40 | Air and Ocean Currents | ☆ |
| 21 | Water in the Air | ☆ | 31 | Past Climates | ☆ | 41 | Rain, Hail, and Snow | ☆ |
| 22 | A Cloudy Sky | ☆ | 32 | Collecting Weather Data | ☆ | 42 | Climate and Climate Change | ☆ |
| 23 | A Cloudy Sky | ☆ | 33 | Collecting Weather Data | ☆ | 43 | Weather Forecasting | ☆ |

# Weather Patterns

Look outside—what is the weather like today? Is it dry or wet, sunny or cloudy, cold or hot? Weather is the state of the atmosphere (the air) all around you at a particular time. Every day, weather affects how you live—what you wear, where you go, what you do. People also rely on the right mixture of weather—sun and rain—to grow crops for food to eat.

## In a day

The weather is the result of a complex mixture of atmospheric conditions. In some places, the weather is quite predictable. In others, it can change dramatically in a few hours, or even faster.

**Sun and rain produce a rainbow**

### Key facts

- In temperate regions (between the tropics and the polar regions), the weather is changeable, with sun and rain in quick succession.
- In tropical regions, daily weather often has a similar pattern, with sunny mornings followed by a brief period of rainfall in the afternoon, and a clear dusk.
- Normal weather in one place may be considered extreme in another. For example, Canada's freezing winters would be considered extreme in Florida.

## Weather systems

Although the weather is very complex, there are patterns of weather across the world. These patterns can be seen clearly from space as layers of clouds. Some weather systems bring rain, while others bring long periods of fine, settled weather. Some, like the monsoon, are seasonal.

### Key facts

- Monsoon winds are strong winds that blow in opposite directions depending on the season.
- Bands of fast-moving air, called jet streams, move high through Earth's atmosphere. The four major jet streams have a huge influence on the world's weather systems below them.

**Bands of clouds above Earth**

## Hottest and coldest

Weather happens in the atmosphere because the sun heats Earth unevenly. The tropical regions near the equator receive more heat energy from the sun than the regions near the poles. The difference in the sun's heat input between the two regions drives the large movements of air that we call wind.

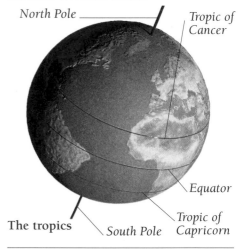

North Pole
Tropic of Cancer
Equator
Tropic of Capricorn
The tropics
South Pole

### Key facts

- The tropics are the regions that lie between the equator and the Tropic of Cancer in the northern hemisphere, and the equator and the Tropic of Capricorn in the southern hemisphere.
- The tropical regions include all the surface area on Earth in which the sun is directly overhead (at 90°) at least once a year.
- The South Pole is colder than the North Pole because the South Pole lies in the middle of the vast Antarctic landmass, while the North Pole is surrounded by the frozen Arctic Ocean.
- Antarctica is covered by a huge sheet of ice that extends over an area of almost 5.4 million sq miles (14 million sq km).

# The Atmosphere

Weather happens in the layer of gases that surround Earth, called the atmosphere. Without the atmosphere, there would be no life on Earth. During the day, the atmosphere prevents us from being burned by some harmful rays from the sun. At night, it stops heat from escaping into space. The world's weather takes place in the lowest part of the atmosphere.

## Above your head

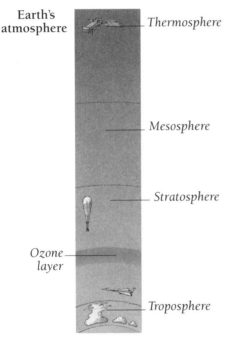

The atmosphere above your head can be divided into several layers (see above). The troposphere is where all the world's weather occurs.

### Key facts

- The troposphere contains about 80 percent of all the gases in the atmosphere and 99 percent of all the water.
- The ozone layer is made up of ozone gas that absorbs harmful ultraviolet rays from the sun.
- Jet planes cruise in the clear air of the stratosphere.

## Atmospheric pressure

The atmosphere is held in place around Earth by the force of gravity. The pull of Earth's gravity means that air presses down on the surface of our planet. The weight of the air pressing down is called atmospheric pressure.

### Key facts

- Atmospheric pressure varies across the surface of Earth according to temperature, giving regions of high and low pressure.
- Atmospheric pressure is measured with an instrument called a barometer. It shows the atmospheric pressure in millibars (mb).
- Atmospheric pressure decreases with height. The higher you climb, the less air there is squashing down from above.

**Aneroid barometer**

## What is air?

The air that we breathe is made up of a mixture of gases. The two main gases are nitrogen and oxygen. Carbon dioxide makes up less than half of 1 percent, yet it is vital for life on Earth as it helps to absorb heat energy from the sun, warming our planet. Other gases include argon, neon, helium, methane, krypton, and hydrogen. The lowest layer of the atmosphere also contains water vapor in the form of an invisible gas.

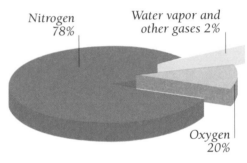

**Pie chart showing percentages of gases that make up Earth's atmosphere**

### Key facts

- Carbon dioxide is called a greenhouse gas because it traps heat around Earth, like the panes of glass in a greenhouse trap heat inside the greenhouse.
- The amount of water vapor in the air around us is called humidity. The more water vapor, the higher the humidity.
- Samples of ice taken deep down from the ice sheets of Greenland and the Antarctic give us information about air from the past 2.7 million years. Tiny air bubbles trapped in the ice are analyzed to give information about the mixture of gases in the air and the temperature of the air.

# The Sun

Sunlight provides the energy that drives the world's weather. The sun's heat keeps Earth's atmosphere in constant motion. Different areas on Earth receive different amounts of heat energy from the sun. It is these variations in heating, from day to night, from season to season, and in different regions, that create the wide variety of weather that humans experience.

## Heat from the sun

Only half if the sun's heat entering Earth's atmosphere reaches the surface of the planet. The rest is either reflected back into space or absorbed by the atmosphere.

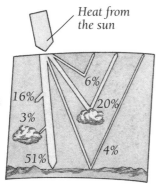

Heat from the sun

What happens to the sun's heat

6%
16%
20%
3%
4%
51%

### Key facts

- Roughly 20 percent of the heat energy from the sun is reflected back to space by clouds. Another 6 percent is reflected by air molecules, and 4 percent is reflected by the surface of Earth.
- Roughly 16 percent of the heat energy from the sun is absorbed by water vapor, and 3 percent is absorbed by clouds.
- The ability of surfaces to reflect energy from the sun is called their albedo. Snow and ice have a very high albedo because they reflect up to 90 percent of the sunlight that hits them.

## The seasons

In the temperate zones (between the tropics and the polar regions), people experience four distinct seasons: winter, spring, summer, and fall. In many tropical areas, there are only two seasons in the year: a dry season and a wet season. In hot desert areas, there are often no seasons at all—it is hot and dry all year round.

### Key facts

**Winter snow**

- As winter draws in, there are fewer hours of sunlight and temperatures drop. Deciduous trees lose their leaves. Many animals start to hibernate.
- During spring, there are more hours of sunlight and temperatures rise. With warmth and sunlight, plants start growing again, and animals come out of hibernation.

## Sun and Earth

As Earth orbits the sun, it spins around on an axis that is tilted slightly from the vertical. It is this tilt of Earth that causes the seasons. In December, the northern hemisphere is tilted away from the sun so it receives less heat energy than the southern hemisphere, which is tilted toward the sun. December is winter in the north and summer in the south. In June, the situation is reversed, with summer in the north and winter in the south.

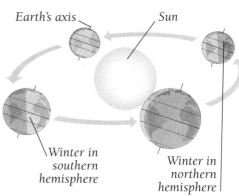

Earth's axis          Sun

Winter in southern hemisphere

Winter in northern hemisphere

### Key facts

- During their winters, the two poles are tilted so far away from the sun that they receive no sunlight at all for several months of the year.
- During their summers, the two poles experience constant daylight. In the Arctic tundra, plants and wildlife flourish in the brief burst of light and warmth.
- When it is winter in the northern hemisphere, the days are short and the nights are long. At the same time, the southern hemisphere is enjoying long days and short nights. Six months later, the situation is reversed.

# Wind

Wind is the movement of air around Earth. Sometimes wind moves gently to give light breezes. At other times, wind can be strong, creating gales, hurricanes, and tornadoes. The movement of wind around our planet is driven by the uneven heating of Earth's surface by the sun, which creates regions of warmer and cooler air. The uneven heating is what sets the air moving.

## The Coriolis effect

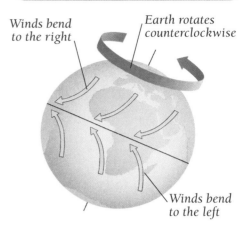

*Winds bend to the right*  
*Earth rotates counterclockwise*  
*Winds bend to the left*

**The rotation of Earth**

If you look at the map of the world's winds, you will see that they do not blow in straight lines from the equator to the poles. This is because Earth is rotating on its axis, and this spinning movement has an effect on the direction of winds.

### Key facts

- In the northern hemisphere, winds blowing toward the equator are bent to the right (toward the west). In the southern hemisphere, winds blowing toward the equator are bent to the left (also toward the west).
- The deflection of winds caused by the rotation of Earth is known as the Coriolis effect after the French scientist Gustave-Gaspard de Coriolis, who described it scientifically in 1835.
- The Coriolis effect is strongest near the poles, and nonexistent at the equator.
- Rotating storms such as hurricanes need the Coriolis effect to start them spinning. Hurricanes cannot start on the equator, because there is no Coriolis effect there.

## The world's winds

As air is warmed, it starts to rise. Because warm air is lighter, it presses down with less force on Earth's surface and creates an area of low pressure. Cool air is more dense than warm air and tends to sink, pressing down with more force and creating areas of high pressure.

### Key facts

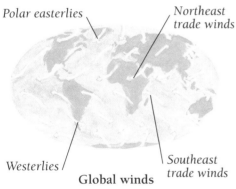

*Polar easterlies*  
*Northeast trade winds*  
*Westerlies*  
*Southeast trade winds*  
**Global winds**

- As warm air rises, cooler air moves in underneath to replace it. Winds blow wherever there are differences in temperature and pressure.
- Winds blow from areas of high pressure to areas of low pressure.
- The world's winds move warm air from the tropics toward the poles. Cold air flows in the opposite direction. This is called general circulation.

## Local winds

In many parts of the world, the wind usually blows from the same direction. This kind of wind is known as the prevailing wind. But in some places, landscape features such as high mountains or steep valleys create smaller, local winds.

### Key facts

- Wind direction is always given as the direction from which the wind is blowing.

**The Mistral whips up snow on Mont Ventoux, France**

- In the tropics, the prevailing winds are known as trade winds because in the days when trade goods were carried around the world in sailing ships, these winds blew the ships westward.
- The Mistral is a local wind that blows down the Rhône Valley in France.

# The Water Cycle

All around us, there is moisture in the air. Even in the driest and hottest desert, the air contains some moisture. This moisture is in the form of an invisible gas called water vapor. Although we can't see water vapor, we can feel it in the air as humidity. If water vapor cools enough in the air, it may turn back into tiny drops of liquid, in a process called condensation.

## Recycling

As the sun's heat warms the surface of Earth, water constantly turns into water vapor (evaporates) in the atmosphere. As the water vapor rises, it cools and turns back into tiny droplets of liquid. Eventually, these tiny droplets may form bigger drops and fall as precipitation.

### Key facts

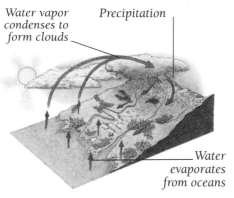

*Water vapor condenses to form clouds*   *Precipitation*

*Water evaporates from oceans*

**The water cycle**

- The process of evaporation and condensation leading to the formation of clouds, rain, and snow is called the water cycle.
- Precipitation is water released from clouds in the form of rain, snow, hail, or sleet.
- Every day, about 1,380 billion tons (1,400 billion metric tons) of precipitation falls on Earth.

## Making clouds

Warm air can hold more water vapor than cold air. On a warm day, the ground heats up and warms the air above it. If one patch of ground becomes warmer than its surrounding area, it may send up a bubble of hot air. As the warm air rises, the water vapor in the air cools and begins to condense. We see the tiny droplets in the air as a cloud.

### Key facts

- Clouds formed in this way are called convection clouds.
- Water vapor condenses into droplets around tiny particles of dust, salt, and smoke that are present in the air, called condensation nuclei.
- The droplets in a cloud are extremely tiny. It takes about 1 million cloud droplets to form one raindrop.

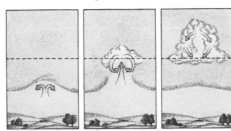

**Cloud formation**

## Rain

**Rain falls from gray clouds**

The droplets in a cloud join together to form bigger drops, and if these drops become large and heavy enough, they may fall as rain. Many falling raindrops do not reach the ground. If they fall through warm, dry air, they may evaporate once more before being carried back up in rising air to condense into clouds again. This effect is known as virga.

### Key facts

- Cloud droplets join together as they bump into each other. This process is called coalescence.
- Most raindrops measure less than $1/5$ in (5 mm) across. Drops that measure less than $1/50$ in (0.5 mm) are classed as drizzle.
- Big raindrops fall more quickly than smaller ones. Drizzle falls so slowly that it often evaporates before it reaches the ground.
- Meteorologists (weather scientists) describe rain as light if less than $1/10$ in (2.5 mm) falls in an hour. Rain is heavy if more than $3/10$ in (7.5 mm) falls in an hour.

# Extreme Weather

Sometimes the weather is extreme, causing devastation and death. Too much rain can cause flooding. No rain and hot weather for extended periods can cause drought. Huge storms with strong winds, such as hurricanes and tornadoes, can wreak widespread damage. Large snowfalls can set off avalanches or be whipped up by high winds into violent blizzards.

## Hurricanes

Hurricanes are the most violent and destructive storms on Earth. They are enormous—the biggest can extend 500 miles (800 km) across. They develop over tropical seas and oceans, as warm, moist air rises off the surface of the water. The winds of a hurricane can blow at up to 185 mph (300 km/h), causing immense damage if the hurricane travels over land.

**A hurricane blows ashore**

### Key facts

- Hurricanes are called tropical cyclones when they occur in the Indian Ocean and south Pacific Ocean, and typhoons in the northwest Pacific Ocean.
- Hurricanes can develop only in regions where the sea temperature is above 80°F (27°C).
- Hurricanes need the Coriolis effect to start spinning.

## Hot weather

When the rainfall drops below the usual level in a particular region for a long time, the result can be drought. Lack of rainfall frequently coincides with extended periods of hot weather, so drought and heat waves are often experienced together. Shortages of water can have devastating consequences for plants, wildife, and people.

### Key facts

- Drought can lead to famine if farmers do not have enough water to grow their crops.
- If the monsoon rains fail to arrive on time in southeast Asia, drought and famine often follow.
- Heat waves are often caused by areas of high pressure that get stuck—called blocking highs.

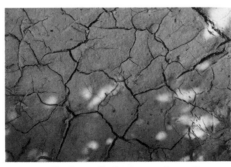

**Parched earth during a drought**

## Snow and ice

Blizzards occur when a snowstorm is driven by high winds or when high winds whip up snow that is lying on the ground. Blizzards often happen in remote or mountainous regions. But when they hit populated places, such as cities, they can cause chaos. Ice storms are a particular hazard in North America. They happen when freezing rain falls, coating everything it touches with a layer of ice. The ice builds up until it is so heavy it snaps branches off trees, drags down power lines, and makes roofs collapse.

**A snowy scene**

### Key facts

- High winds can blow snow into deep piles called snowdrifts. Snowdrifts up to 40 ft (12 m) high can bury cars and houses, trap livestock, and make moving around impossible.
- During an ice storm, the ice can build up to thicknesses of 6 in (15 cm) or more.
- An ice storm that devastated eastern Canada and the northeastern United States in 1998 is one of the worst natural disasters ever to hit Canada.

# Climate Change

Throughout Earth's history, the world's climate has varied from time to time. The biggest changes have occurred between very cold periods, called ice ages, and warmer periods, called interglacials. The most recent ice age ended about 11,500 years ago, and we are now in an interglacial. Today, human activity is further warming our planet and having a major impact on its climate.

## Greenhouse effect

Greenhouse gases such as water vapor, carbon dioxide, and methane trap heat around Earth, helping keep our planet warm. But burning fossil fuels such as oil, natural gas, and coal has increased the amount of carbon dioxide in the atmosphere. The increase in greenhouse gases means that more heat is being trapped in Earth's atmosphere, causing global warming.

### Key facts

- Fossil fuels are the fossilized remains of plants and animals from many millions of years ago. These fuels release carbon dioxide into the atmosphere.

- Methane from cattle, swamps, and garbage tips accounts for about 25 percent of the greenhouse effect.

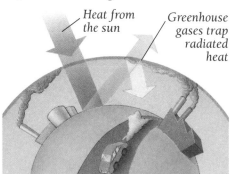

*Heat from the sun*  *Greenhouse gases trap radiated heat*

**Warming our planet**

## The ozone hole

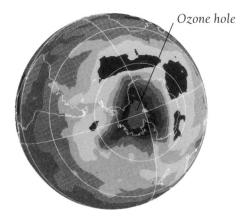

*Ozone hole*

**Ozone hole over Antarctica**

Ozone is a gas that helps prevent harmful rays from the sun from reaching Earth. These rays can cause skin cancer and slow plant growth. In 1983, scientists identified a hole in the ozone layer above Antarctica.

### Key facts

- Ozone levels in the atmosphere reached a low in the 1990s and have increased again since then.

- The fall in ozone levels was caused by chlorofluorocarbons (CFCs). These chemicals are no longer used in aerosols and fridges.

- In 2019, it was found that the ozone hole was smaller than at any time since 1982.

## How hot?

The increase in greenhouse gases in Earth's atmosphere is making the world heat up—an effect called global warming. Scientists predict that unless drastic action is taken, the world will warm by about another 3.6°F (2.0°C) by the year 2100. This would have major impacts around the globe, including a devastating rise in sea level, more heat waves, wildfires, and hurricanes, and major damage to coral reefs.

### Key facts

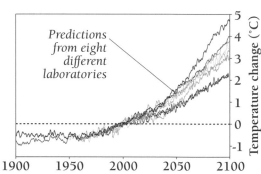

*Predictions from eight different laboratories*

**Global warming predictions**

- Higher temperatures in the polar regions are melting vast areas of ice sheets in the Arctic and Antarctic. As the ice melts, the released water flows into the oceans, causing sea levels to rise.

- If the ice at the North Pole continues to melt at its present rate, there will be no summer ice remaining by 2050.

- Rising sea levels are likely to submerge many low-lying islands and coastal regions.

- To slow climate change, people need to greatly reduce the burning of fossil fuels.

# Forecasting

Weather scientists called meteorologists use powerful computers to predict what the weather will do over the next 24 hours, and longer term. Measurements from a wide range of sources are fed into these computers, to try to give as accurate a picture as possible. Information about the weather is collected from weather stations all over the world, and from orbiting satellites.

## Satellite pictures

Data from satellites plays a vital part in piecing together what is happening to the world's weather. Weather satellites are carried into space by unmanned rockets, which send the satellites into orbit around Earth.

### Key facts

- Some weather satellites are geostationary. They orbit Earth at a height of (22,400 miles (36,000 km). At this height, they remain above the same place on the ground all the time.

- Other weather satellites are polar orbiting satellites. They orbit at a height of roughly 530 miles (850 km) and pass over each pole several times every day.

- Weather satellites transmit information about temperature, clouds, and wind back to Earth.

Satellite image of hurricane

## Weather balloons

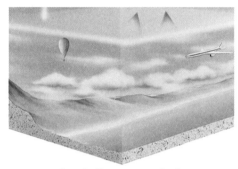
Weather balloons rise high into the atmosphere

Weather balloons are sent high into Earth's atmosphere. These balloons are filled with hydrogen gas and reach heights of 25 miles (40 km) before they disintegrate. They carry instruments that send information back to meteorologists on Earth.

### Key facts

- Weather balloons are released twice a day from almost 800 different locations worldwide.

- Weather balloons can drift as far as 125 miles (200 km) from their launching place. By tracking a balloon, meteorologists can calculate wind speed.

- The package of instruments attached to a weather balloon is called the radiosonde.

## Why is it important?

We all like to know what the weather is going to do—whether it will be rainy or sunny and whether we need to take an umbrella when we go out in the morning. But for some people, the weather forecast is vitally important. Coastguardsmen, fishermen, and sailors rely on weather forecasts to know what the conditions are likely to be at sea. Farmers need to know how the weather is likely to affect their crops. Pilots and air traffic controllers rely on weather forecasts to guide planes away from storms and other hazards.

Weather forecasts are vital for sailors

### Key facts

- Weather forecasts are issued in many different forms. There are weather reports in newspapers and websites, as well as on TV and radio, and weather apps downloadable to smartphones.

- Many countries broadcast special weather forecasts for sailors and farmers.

- If extreme weather is predicted, such as a blizzard or a hurricane, meteorologists issue an alert to warn people in the affected areas.

# The World's Climates

Climate is the average weather experienced in a particular place over a length of time. The coldest climates on Earth are found near the two poles, and the hottest climates in the tropics near the equator. Some places, such as deserts, have very dry climates, while others, such as rain forest regions, are hot and wet all year round.

## Which climate?

*This map shows the world's different climate zones. Use the information on the charts at the back of the book to fill in the blank spaces in the map key.*

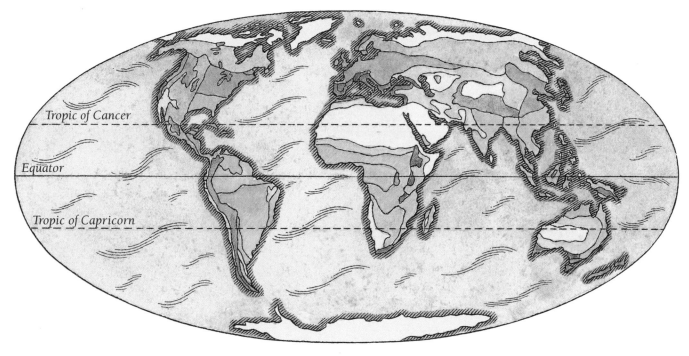

| Key | Zone | Seasons |
|---|---|---|
| | 1. Mountain | Climate depends on altitude (see page 28) |
| | 2. Taiga | ............................................... |
| | 3. ................................................ | Extreme cold all year round |
| | 4. ................................................ | Warm summers; mild winters |
| | 5. Mediterranean | ............................................... |
| | 6. ................................................ | Dry hot summers; cold winters |
| | 7. ................................................ | Hot summers; mild winters |
| | 8. Tropical | ............................................... |
| | 9. ................................................ | Dry and hot all year round |

## Climate adaptations

*Plants and animals have adapted to live in some of the world's harshest climates. Match the images and their descriptions to the correct names from the list on the right.*

*Choose from:*

**Rain forest tree** **Penguin** **Camel** **Snow leopard**
**Coniferous tree** **Cactus**

1. .................

This animal can survive for days without water.

2. ......................

This bird has a layer of fat, called blubber, to keep it warm.

3. ..............................................

This animal has thick hair to keep it warm in its cold mountain habitat.

6. ......................

4. ..............................................

This plant grows quickly in the hot and wet rain forests of South America.

5. ..............................................

The thin needles of this evergreen tree have a waxy coating to protect them in cold climates.

This plant stores water in its stem. Its leaves are sharp spines that help shade it from the hot sun.

## Homes and climate

*The climate of a particular region affects the types of homes in which people live. Fill in the missing words in these descriptions, using the pictures to help you.*

1. In Africa and other places with hot, dry climates, people have built houses out of ...................... for centuries. The thick walls help keep the inside of the house cool.

2. In the frozen Arctic, the Inuit people know how to build shelters out of blocks of snow. These shelters are called ......................

3. On the steppes of Central Asia, the climate can be very cold. Some people live in movable houses made out of frames covered with thick felt. These cozy tents are called ......................

4. In temperate climates, it often rains. People build houses with steep ...................... so that the rainwater can run off easily.

**Igloo**

**Steep-roofed houses**

**Mud house**

**Yurt**

# Light from the Sun

Heat from the sun drives the weather that swirls around Earth. But because Earth's surface is curved, the sun heats Earth unevenly. In the tropics, the sun's rays strike Earth's surface directly, concentrating the heat energy. At the poles, the sun's rays strike at more of an angle, spreading the heat energy over a larger area.

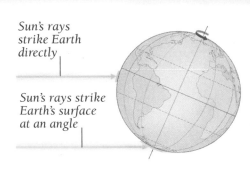

*Sun's rays strike Earth directly*

*Sun's rays strike Earth's surface at an angle*

**How the sun's rays strike Earth**

## See for yourself

*Try this experiment to see for yourself why the sun heats Earth unevenly.*

1 Hold a flashlight so that the light beam shines directly down on a piece of white paper and trace the shape of the lit area on the paper.

2 Now hold the flashlight so that the light beam shines at an angle on the paper and trace the shape again. Which shape is bigger?

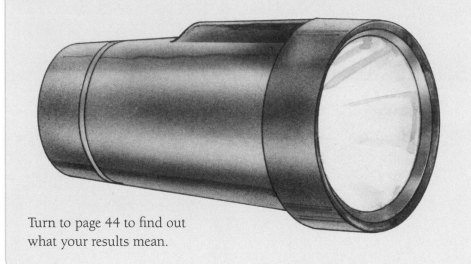

Turn to page 44 to find out what your results mean.

## Sun spectaculars

- Pure white sunlight is actually a mixture of colors.
- When sunlight falls on rain, the raindrops bend and separate the light into the seven colors of the rainbow.

- At sunset, we often see red, orange, and yellow skies. The sun is so low in the sky that the dense atmosphere scatters the green, blue, indigo, and violet rays.

## Sun test

*Circle the correct words to complete the statements below. Use the information on page 8 and on this page to help you.*

1. About one- **half / quarter** of the sun's heat energy entering Earth's atmosphere actually reaches the ground to heat the oceans and continents.

2. The ability of a surface to reflect sunlight is called its **albino / albedo**.

3. At the equator, the sun's rays strike Earth **more / less directly** than at the poles.

4. In June the North Pole is tilted **toward / away from** the sun.

5. A rainbow is caused by raindrops splitting sunlight into **seven / nine** separate colors.

6. At sunset, the sky is often **reddish-orange / blue-green** because the dense atmosphere scatters some of the sun's rays.

# Ocean Currents

Heat energy from the sun drives ocean currents. The vast oceans carry heat from the tropics toward the polar regions, while cold currents from the poles help cool the tropics. The oceans also warm up and lose heat more slowly than land, making coastal climates less extreme than the climates experienced far away from the coasts.

> ### Did you know?
> All the world's ocean currents are linked together in a vast system that redistributes heat energy around Earth. This system is known as the ocean conveyor belt, because it moves in a giant loop.

## Naming currents

*Read the descriptions of these ocean currents. Then write the correct number in the boxes to identify each current.*

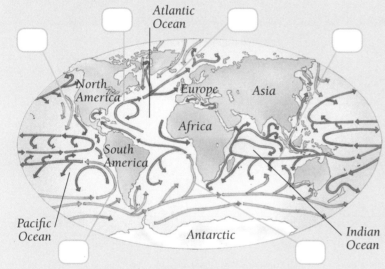

1. **Gulf Stream** carries warm water from the Gulf of Mexico into the North Atlantic.

2. **Humboldt Current** carries cold water from the Antarctic northward along the west coast of South America.

3. **Benguela Current** carries cold water from the Antarctic northward along the west coast of Africa.

4. **North Atlantic Drift** continues carrying the warm waters of the Gulf Stream along the coast of northwest Europe.

5. **California Current** carries cold water southward along the western North American coast.

6. **South Equatorial Current** is a significant Pacific, Atlantic, and Indian ocean current that flows east to west between the equator and about 20° south.

## El Niño

*Read the information about El Niño below. Then draw a line to link each caption to the correct part of the picture, which shows the situation during an El Niño event.*

In the Pacific Ocean, the warm South Equatorial current normally flows from east to west. It draws cold water up from the ocean floor along the South American coast. In Australia and southeast Asia, water vapor rises from the warm oceans and fuels heavy rain. Every two to five years, there is a change to this usual pattern of ocean currents and air circulation, called El Niño.

**During El Niño:**

4. **Australia and southeast Asia often suffer from drought.**

3. **Warm surface water causes heavy rain in South America.**

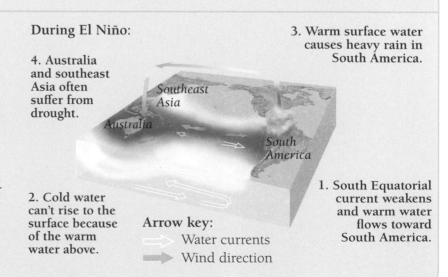

2. **Cold water can't rise to the surface because of the warm water above.**

1. **South Equatorial current weakens and warm water flows toward South America.**

**Arrow key:**
⟹ Water currents
⟹ Wind direction

# A Windy Day

Meteorologists measure the wind to find out what direction it is blowing from and the speed at which it is blowing. Wind vanes indicate wind direction. Instruments called anemometers measure wind speed. To describe wind speed, and its likely effects, meteorologists use the Beaufort scale.

### Did you know?

The Beaufort scale is named after its creator, an officer in the British navy called Sir Francis Beaufort. He developed the scale in 1805 as an accurate method of describing the force of the wind.

## Measuring wind speed

*You can make a simple anemometer to measure the speed of the wind.*

**1** Tie a piece of cotton thread to the middle of a protractor. Tape the other end of the thread to a table tennis ball.

**2** Check that the thread hangs straight down in still air. This indicates a speed of 0 mph (0 km/h).

**3** Hold the anemometer parallel to the wind so that the ball is blown sideways. By reading the angle of the thread on the protractor, you can estimate the strength of the wind.

**4** Compare your wind speed readings with the wind strengths on the Beaufort scale below. What was the highest wind force you measured?

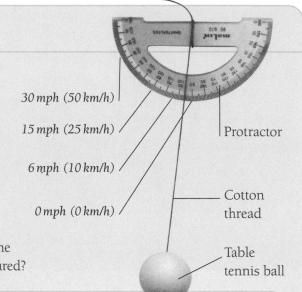

30 mph (50 km/h)

15 mph (25 km/h)

6 mph (10 km/h)

0 mph (0 km/h)

Protractor

Cotton thread

Table tennis ball

| Force | Description | Wind speed mph (km/h) | Effects |
|---|---|---|---|
| 0 | Calm | 0.1 or less (0.2 or less) | Smoke rises vertically |
| 1 | Light air | 1–3 (2–5) | Wind vanes and flags do not move, but rising smoke drifts |
| 2 | Light breeze | 4–7 (6–11) | Drifting smoke indicates the wind direction |
| 3 | Gentle breeze | 8–12 (12–19) | Leaves rustle, small twigs move, and lightweight flags stir gently |
| 4 | Moderate breeze | 13–18 (20–29) | Loose leaves and pieces of paper blow around |
| 5 | Fresh breeze | 19–24 (30–39) | Small trees in leaf begin to sway |
| 6 | Strong breeze | 25–31 (40–50) | Umbrellas used with difficulty |
| 7 | Moderate gale | 32–38 (51–62) | The wind exerts strong pressure on people walking into it |
| 8 | Gale | 39–46 (63–75) | Twigs break off trees |
| 9 | Strong gale | 47–54 (76–87) | Chimneys blown down; slates and tiles torn from roofs |
| 10 | Storm | 55–63 (88–102) | Trees uprooted; considerable structural damage |
| 11 | Violent storm | 64–75 (103–120) | Rarely experienced—widespread devastation, buildings destroyed |
| 12+ | Hurricane | 75 or more (120 or more) | |

# What is wind chill?

*The strength of the wind can affect your body temperature. The wind blows away the thin layer of air warmed by your body, making you feel cold. Although the actual air temperature remains the same, wind chill can make it feel much colder.*

Look at the wind chill table below. To figure out the wind chill temperature, find the actual air temperature (along the top) and the wind speed (down the side). Work down from the temperature and across from the wind speed until you find the place where the two meet. This tells you the wind chill caused by this combination of air temperature and wind.

1. If the air temperature is 41°F and the wind speed is 22 mph, what is the wind chill temperature? .........

2. If the wind speed is 16 mph and the air temperature is 14°F, what is the wind chill temperature? .........

3. If the wind chill temperature is −15°F and the wind speed is 19 mph, what is the actual air temperature? ............

4. If the air temperature is 23°F and the wind chill temperature is 12°F, what is the wind speed? ............

|  |  | Temperature °F | | | | | | |
|---|---|---|---|---|---|---|---|---|
|  |  | 50 | 41 | 32 | 23 | 14 | 5 | 4 |
| | 0 | 50 | 41 | 32 | 23 | 14 | 5 | 4 |
| | 3 | 50 | 39 | 28 | 19 | 9 | −2 | −11 |
| | 6 | 48 | 37 | 27 | 16 | 5 | −6 | −17 |
| | 9 | 46 | 36 | 25 | 12 | 1 | −9 | −20 |
| Wind speed mph | 12 | 45 | 34 | 23 | 10 | 0.5 | −24 | −22 |
| | 16 | 45 | 34 | 21 | 10 | −2 | −11 | −26 |
| | 19 | 45 | 32 | 21 | 9 | −4 | −15 | −27 |
| | 22 | 43 | 32 | 19 | 7 | −4 | −17 | −27 |
| | 25 | 43 | 30 | 19 | 7 | −6 | −17 | −29 |
| | 28 | 43 | 30 | 18 | 5 | −6 | −18 | −31 |
| | 31 | 43 | 30 | 18 | 5 | −8 | −20 | −31 |

# Twister puzzle

*Read the facts about tornadoes, then fill in the missing labels on the picture. Choose from:*

**wall cloud    funnel    devastation**

- Tornadoes are spinning columns of air that form beneath thunderclouds (cumulonimbus). Because they are spinning storms, they are sometimes known as twisters.

- Tornadoes form out of a wall cloud at the base of the thundercloud. The spinning column of air, called the funnel, extends down from the wall cloud until it touches the ground.

- The winds inside a tornado are the fastest on Earth. As tornadoes move across the ground, they can cause great devastation, destroying buildings, uprooting trees, and flinging vehicles around.

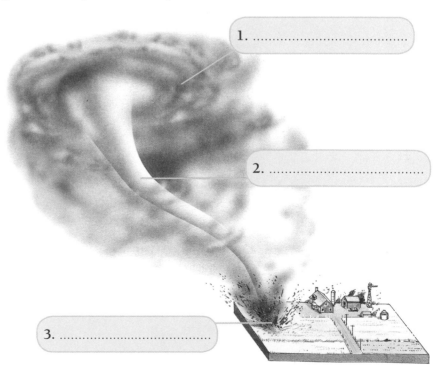

1. ....................................

2. ....................................

3. ....................................

# Warm and Cold

As air circulates in Earth's atmosphere, it is affected by whether it is passing over land (continental) or over the sea (maritime). Air that is over cold land tends to cool, while hot land heats the air above. Air that is over the sea picks up moisture. Large bodies of air with similar characteristics are called air masses.

## Masses of air

*Read the information about the four main types of air masses. Then number the boxes on the diagram to correspond with the descriptions of the different kinds of air masses.*

### Did you know?

On weather maps, a warm front is indicated by a line with red semicircles, and a cold front by a line with blue triangles.

### Air mass facts

Air masses are defined mainly by their temperature and their moisture content. There are four main types of air masses:

1. Tropical continental (Tc)— warm and dry over land.
2. Tropical maritime (Tm)— warm and moist over oceans.
3. Polar continental (Pc)—cold and dry over land.
4. Polar maritime (Pm)—cold and moist over oceans.

## Warm and cold fronts

*When two air masses meet, they do not mix, because one is usually colder than the other. Read the descriptions below, then fill in the missing labels on the diagrams using the words in bold in the descriptions.*

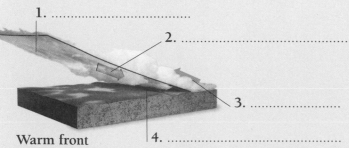

1. ............................................
2. ..................................................
3. .......................
4. .................................................

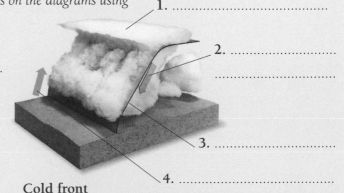

1. ...............................................
2. ............................
   ............................
3. ............................
4. ...........................................

**Warm front**
When a warm air mass meets a cooler air mass, the less dense, **warmer air rises** up above the **denser, cooler air**. As the warm air rises, it cools and condenses, forming **clouds**. Warm fronts often bring clouds and steady **rain**.

**Cold front**
At a cold front, the **dense, cold air** pushes up the **warmer air** to create a **steep slope**. The warm air rises and condenses quickly, often creating **storm clouds** along the front.

# Water in the Air

Water is constantly evaporating from Earth's surface into the air above. Eventually, this water falls back to Earth as precipitation—rain, snow, hail, or sleet. Meteorologists measure the amount of rainfall using a rain gauge. In many regions of the world, people rely on regular seasonal rainfall to water their crops.

## Monsoon facts

- The Asian monsoon brings seasonal rainfall to Pakistan, India, and southeast Asia.

- During winter, this region experiences a dry season when high pressure over the Asian continent and low pressure over the Indian Ocean create cool, dry northeast winds.

- During summer, the land warms up faster than the sea, creating a low-pressure area over the land. The southwest monsoon brings warm, wet air and torrential rain from the Indian Ocean.

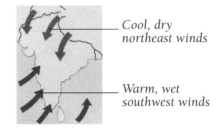

*Cool, dry northeast winds*

*Warm, wet southwest winds*

## True or false?

*Read the following sentences about the monsoon. Using the information on this page and page 9, check the boxes to show which facts are true or false.*

|  | TRUE | FALSE |
|---|---|---|
| 1. Winds blow from areas of low pressure to areas of high pressure. | ☐ | ☐ |
| 2. The dry season in India is caused by the northeast monsoon wind. | ☐ | ☐ |
| 3. The wind that brings rainfall to southeast Asia comes from the Pacific Ocean. | ☐ | ☐ |
| 4. In the summer, land heats up more quickly than the sea. | ☐ | ☐ |
| 5. Rising warm air creates an area of high pressure. | ☐ | ☐ |

## How much rain?

*You can make a simple rain gauge using a jar, a funnel, and a ruler.*

1 Place the funnel into the top of the jar.

2 Tape the ruler to the side of the jar.

3 Add water to the jar up to the level of 0 mm. Then put your rain gauge outside.

4 Check your rain gauge every day at the same time and note down the amount of water in the jar above the 0 mm mark.

5 After a week, return the water level to the 0 mm mark and start a new set of measurements.

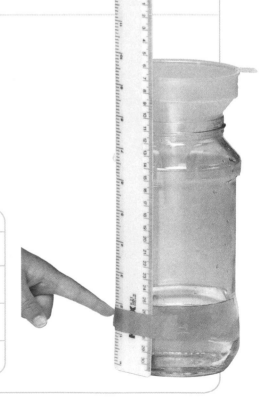

|  | Sun | Mon | Tues | Wed | Thurs | Fri | Sat | Total |
|---|---|---|---|---|---|---|---|---|
| Week 1 |  |  |  |  |  |  |  |  |
| Week 2 |  |  |  |  |  |  |  |  |
| Week 3 |  |  |  |  |  |  |  |  |
| Week 4 |  |  |  |  |  |  |  |  |

# A Cloudy Sky

Clouds range from fluffy cumulus to wispy cirrus, but all clouds are made of the same ingredients. Low-level clouds are formed by tiny water droplets. At high altitudes, where the temperature is below freezing, the water droplets condense and freeze to make ice crystals.

## Keep a cloud chart

 **WARNING** Never point your camera or look directly at the sun.

*Observe the sky and record when you see the 10 main cloud types below. Use the facts box on page 23 to help you.*

*What type of weather do the different clouds bring? You could also build up your own photo library of clouds.*

| Cloud type | Date seen | Time seen | Weather conditions |
|---|---|---|---|
| Cirrus | | | |
| Cirrostratus | | | |
| Cirrocumulus | | | |
| Altostratus | | | |
| Altocumulus | | | |

| Cloud type | Date seen | Time seen | Weather conditions |
|---|---|---|---|
| Stratocumulus | | | |
| Cumulus | | | |
| Cumulonimbus | | | |
| Stratus | | | |
| Nimbostratus | | | |

# Cloud name activity

*Using the information on this page and the pictures on page 22 to help you, fill in the missing words in the sentences below. Choose from:*

**Nimbostratus   Cumulonimbus   Stratus   Cirrus**

1. ......................... are high-level wispy clouds that are sometimes called mares' tails and usually indicate fair weather.

2. Mid-level storm clouds that often bring rain or snow are called ....................................

3. ......................... is a low-level sheet of gray, featureless cloud that obscures the sun during the day.

4. .......................................... clouds are thunderclouds that rise to great heights.

# Match the sky

*The sky can often give you a good indication of the weather to come. Read the captions below about what each of these skies means, then write the correct number against each picture.*

1. Cirrocumulus and altocumulus can form a pattern that is often known as "mackerel sky" because it looks like the stripes on the back of a mackerel. This sky is usually a warning of cloudier and rainier weather to come.

2. "Red sky at night, shepherd's delight. Red sky in the morning, shepherd's warning." Red skies at sunrise often warn of bad weather to come.

3. Tall cumulus clouds that look a bit like giant cauliflowers often produce showers.

# Cloud facts

- High-level clouds include cirrus (wispy clouds), cirrocumulus (tiny cloudlets), and cirrostratus (sheet cloud). They occur near the top of the troposphere at 20,000–46,000 ft (6,000–14,000 m) above Earth's surface.

- Mid-level clouds include altocumulus (small, puffy clouds), altostratus (sheet cloud), and nimbostratus (thick rain cloud). These clouds occur at a height of 6,500–20,000 ft (2,000–6,000 m), although nimbostratus clouds can extend lower.

- Low-level clouds include cumulus (white fluffy clouds), stratocumulus (lumpy, gray cloud), and stratus (gray, featureless cloud). These clouds occur at less than 6,500 ft (2,000 m), above Earth's surface.

- Cumulonimbus are classed as low-level clouds, because their bottoms usually lie below 6,500 ft (2,000 m), but they can extend to the top of the troposphere and may be more than 33,000 ft (10,000 m) high. These clouds often bring thunderstorms and heavy rain.

# Did you know?

As airplanes fly through the stratosphere, their engines leave trails of water vapor across the sky. At such high altitudes, the water vapor freezes almost immediately, leaving visible trails known as contrails.

# Stormy Times

Hurricanes are violent tropical storms. They develop over warm oceans and seas where vast quantities of water evaporate off the surface, rising and eventually turning into gigantic cumulonimbus clouds. Air rushes into the area of low atmospheric pressure just above the surface of the water, creating winds that blow in a circular pattern. This is the beginning of a hurricane.

## How a hurricane works

*Read about the main features of a hurricane below.*
*Then number the diagram 1 to 7 to match up with the descriptions.*

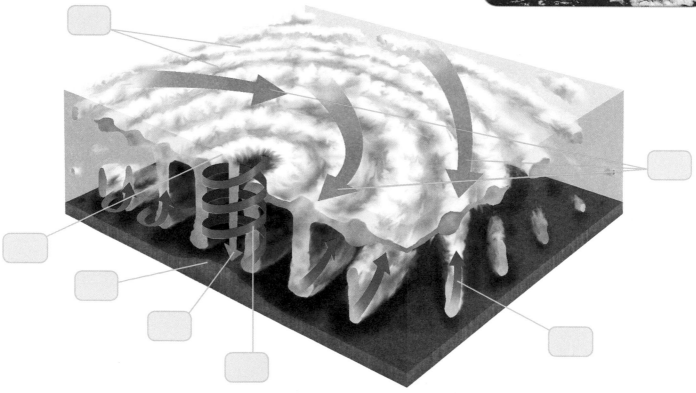

## Hurricane features

1. At the centre of a hurricane is an area of extremely low pressure called the **eye**, with little or no wind.

2. Around the eye is a circle of cloud called the **eyewall**.

3. The eyewall is where the **strongest winds** of the hurricane spiral upward with speeds of up to 200 mph (320 km/h).

4. The extremely low pressure in the eye and the high pressure around it causes a bulge of water in the eye, called a **storm surge**.

5. **Warm air** moves upward.

6. Dense clouds form in **spiral cloud bands,** which often produce huge amounts of rain.

7. **High-level winds** spread out at the top of the storm to create a vast swirl of clouds.

# Thunder and Lightning

Thunderstorms are the most common form of violent weather on Earth. They are unleashed from giant cumulonimbus clouds and can cause terrible damage. Inside a cumulonimbus cloud, rapidly rising warm air and sinking cooler air create powerful air currents that surge up and down, pulling water droplets, ice crystals, and hailstones with them. These are the conditions that can lead to thunder and lightning.

## True or false?

*Read the following sentences about thunder and lightning. Using the information on this page, check the boxes to show which facts are true and which are false.*

|  | TRUE | FALSE |
|---|---|---|
| 1. Cumulus clouds are the clouds that produce thunderstorms. | ☐ | ☐ |
| 2. Inside a thundercloud, water droplets, ice crystals, and hailstones whirl up and down. | ☐ | ☐ |
| 3. Negatively charged particles pile up at the top of the cloud. | ☐ | ☐ |
| 4. The charges at the bottom of the cloud cause the ground to become positively charged. | ☐ | ☐ |
| 5. Lightning can occur within the cloud. | ☐ | ☐ |

## Lightning facts

- As water droplets, ice crystals, and hailstones whirl up and down in a thundercloud, they become electrically charged.
- Lighter, positively charged ice crystals and water droplets pile up at the top of the cloud.
- Heavier, negatively charged hail and water droplets accumulate at the bottom of the cloud, causing the ground to become positively charged.
- When the difference between the opposite charges becomes too great, the energy is discharged in lightning, either in the cloud or between the cloud and the ground.
- Lightning and thunder occur at the same time, but sound waves from thunder take longer to reach us than light from lightning. This explains why we often see lightning before we hear thunder.

## What is lightning?

*Complete each of these sentences below, using the information from the pictures.*

1. The first discharge, or flow, of electricity from the base of the cloud to the nearest high point on the ground below is called the ...............................
2. This discharge creates a channel along which electricity can flow. It is followed immediately by the ...................................................., which shoots back up to the cloud.
3. The air along the path of the lightning is heated massively, causing a .................................... We hear this as thunder.
4. There may be ............................... of lightning along the path of the leader and the return stroke in a fraction of a second. They are so fast that we see them as flickering lightning.

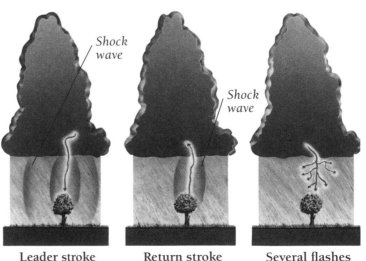

*Shock wave*

*Shock wave*

**Leader stroke**   **Return stroke**   **Several flashes**

# Hail and Snow

Giant cumulonimbus clouds not only produce thunder and lightning, but they can also hurl hailstones down to earth. Hailstones are generally smaller than 1 in (2.5 cm) in diameter, but sometimes they can grow into the size of oranges—or even bigger—before they fall to the ground. Snow is made from tiny ice crystals and is therefore much lighter than hail.

## Making hail

*Read the steps describing how hail is formed inside a thundercloud. Then look at the diagram and number the boxes to match up with each stage of the process.*

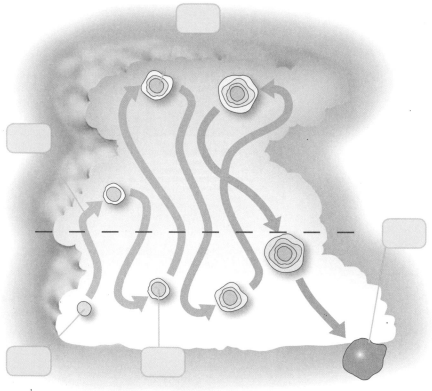

1. Hailstones start life as frozen water droplets or snow pellets called hail embryos.
2. The powerful air currents in a cumulonimbus cloud carry the hail embryo up and down.
3. At the bottom of the cloud, the hail embryo becomes covered in a layer of moisture that freezes as the hail embryo whirls upward.
4. At the top of the cloud, the hail embryo is covered in a layer of ice.
5. The hail embryo gets bigger and bigger until it is so heavy it drops to the ground as a hailstone.

## Snow facts

- Snow is made from tiny ice crystals that stick together to form snowflakes.
- Snowflakes are six-sided and symmetrical, and no two snowflakes are identical.
- Wet snow occurs at around freezing point. The snowflakes are covered with a thin film of water that melts and refreezes easily, making this type of snow very slippery.
- Dry snow occurs at very low temperatures. The water in this type of snow is frozen solid, so dry snow does not stick together as well as wet snow.
- Sleet is wet snow and rain.

## Snow test

*Read the information about snow on page 11 and on this page. Then circle the correct word to complete each sentence.*

1. Snowflakes are made from tiny **ice crystals / water droplets**.
2. Snowflakes have **six / eight** sides and are all **identical / different**.
3. When snow is blown by the wind into a huge mound it is called a **snowpile / snowdrift**.
4. Places such as Antarctica that experience very low temperatures tend to have **dry / wet** snow.
5. Wet snow is usually **very / not very** slippery.

# Fog and Frost

When clouds form at ground level, we call them fog or mist. In a fog, the air is filled with tiny water droplets, making it difficult to see very far. Fog and mist are formed in the same way, but fog is usually thicker than mist. In winter, temperatures near the ground can fall so low that water vapor in the air freezes, forming white crystals called frost.

## Fog facts

- Mist and fog are formed when moist air containing water vapor cools and condenses into visible water droplets.
- Radiation fog happens on clear nights when there is no blanket of cloud to trap heat near the ground. The heat radiates (escapes) into space and the ground cools down, turning any moisture in the air into water droplets and producing fog.
- Advection fog happens when warm, moist air moves over cold land or water. The air cools and the moisture condenses into fog.
- In mist, objects as far as 3,280 ft (1,000 m) away can be seen. In fog, the visibility is worse.

## True or false?

*Read the following sentences about fog. Using the information on this page, check the boxes to show which facts are true and which are false.*

| | TRUE | FALSE |
|---|---|---|
| 1. Mist is thicker than fog. | ☐ | ☐ |
| 2. Fog and mist are ground-level clouds. | ☐ | ☐ |
| 3. Fog and mist happen when water vapor in the air evaporates. | ☐ | ☐ |
| 4. Radiation fog typically happens on cloudy, windy nights. | ☐ | ☐ |
| 5. Advection fog is the result of warm, moist air meeting a cold surface. | ☐ | ☐ |
| 6. In fog, visibility is less than 3,280 ft (1,000 m). In mist, objects at this distance can be seen. | ☐ | ☐ |

## Frost puzzle

*Look at the pictures of different types of frost, then match the descriptions to the correct picture.*

1.

2.

3.

**a.** Frost that forms beautiful patterns on windows is called **fern frost**.

**b.** Tiny ice crystals that cover every surface with a glittering white are called **hoar frost**.

**c.** When ice crystals build up on solid objects to form a white crust, it is called **rime frost**.

# Mountain Weather

Mountains reach high into Earth's atmosphere. Some are so tall that their tops are often above the clouds that fill the valleys around them. Mountains have an effect on the weather because they force air to move up and down. They also have their own unique climates, which change according to altitude (height above sea level).

## Rain shadow puzzle

*Read these steps describing the rain shadow effect. Then look carefully at the diagram below and number the boxes to match up with each step.*

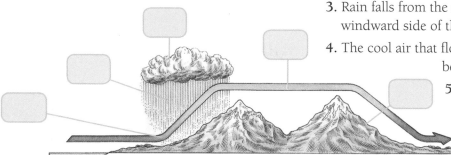

1. When moist, warm air moves toward a mountain range, it is forced upward.

2. As the air rises, it cools and condenses, forming clouds.

3. Rain falls from the clouds, making the slopes on the windward side of the mountain very wet.

4. The cool air that flows across the mountains is dry because it has lost its moisture.

5. The leeward side of the mountain is usually much drier than the windward side. This is known as the rain shadow effect.

## Mountain zones

*The climate, vegetation, and wildlife on a mountain change according to altitude. Read the descriptions of the climate zones on this picture of a mountain in the Himalayas. Then fill in the missing words from the list below.*

*Choose from:*

**alpine   altitude   deciduous
mountain   red panda   tree line**

The lammergeier (or bearded vulture) lives among the .................. peaks and feeds off carcasses of dead animals.

High .............. grasslands provide food for takin during the summer.

The coniferous forests lie above the deciduous forests in a slightly cooler climate zone. They are home to animals such as the ....... ..............

The snow leopard is one of the few animals that can survive in the tundra regions at high ..................

The ........ ............. —the point where the climate becomes too cold for trees to survive—is at roughly 11,200 ft (3,400 m). Above this are high grasslands where wild ass graze during the summer.

At the base of the Himalayas, the climate is subtropical with .................. forests that are home to animals such as the Nepal gray langur.

# Land and Sea

The land heats up and loses heat more quickly than the sea. Because of this difference, climates in coastal areas are generally much less extreme than climates in places far away from the sea. In the winter, the sea remains relatively warm compared to the land, while in the summer it remains relatively cool.

## Coastal weather test

*Circle the correct word to complete each sentence, using the information on this page to help you.*

1. During the day, it can be quite windy at the seaside because of **land / sea** breezes.
2. Sea fogs are usually **radiation / advection** fogs.
3. Moist prevailing winds blowing off the sea often bring **dry / wet** conditions to coastal areas.
4. A maritime climate tends to have **mild / very cold** winters and **very hot / warm** summers.

A foggy coastline

## Coastal facts

- Coasts are often quite windy, with sea breezes in the daytime and land breezes at night. There are no obstacles across the open sea to stop the wind from blowing hard.
- Sea fogs can be a problem for ships. These fogs are advection fogs, caused by warm air blowing over cooler water. Sometimes sea fogs can linger for days.
- Coastal areas can be quite rainy, especially if they face into the prevailing wind.
- The climate of coastal regions is known as a maritime climate, because it is affected by the sea.
- The strong winds that blow across the world's oceans help carry seabirds such as albatrosses over vast distances.

## Land and sea breezes

*Look closely at the diagrams on the right, then complete each of these sentences using the information on this page.*

1. During the day, the .................. warms up more quickly than the ..................
2. During the day, warm air rises from the land, drawing in ..................air from the sea. This is called a sea breeze.
3. During the night, the land .................................. more quickly than the sea.
4. During the night, .................. air rises from the sea, drawing in cool air from the land. This is called a land breeze.

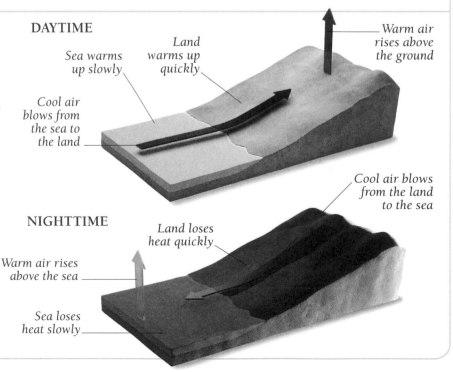

**DAYTIME**

Sea warms up slowly

Land warms up quickly

Warm air rises above the ground

Cool air blows from the sea to the land

**NIGHTTIME**

Land loses heat quickly

Warm air rises above the sea

Cool air blows from the land to the sea

Sea loses heat slowly

# Weathering and Erosion

The weather has a direct impact on the landscape around us. In places such as deserts, which have very hot days and very cold nights, the daily difference in temperature can cause rocks to shatter. In mountain regions, moisture lying on the ground continually freezes and thaws, creating cracks and crevices in rocks. These processes are known as weathering.

## Water to ice

*What happens when rainwater seeps into tiny cracks in rocks then freezes? Do this simple activity to find out why the process of freezing, thawing, and freezing again gradually widens cracks in rocks, sometimes shattering the rocks into small fragments..*

**1** Fill two jars half full with water. Mark the water level on the jars with a piece of tape.

**2** Put one jar in the freezer until the water freezes. Then compare the level of the ice with the water in the unfrozen jar. Are the levels still the same?................

## Erosion quiz

*Read the glacial erosion facts. Then circle the correct words to complete each sentence below.*

1. In high mountain regions, the summer sun melts **some of / all of** the snow.
2. A glacier is formed as the accumulated snow turns into **ice / water.**
3. A glacier moves very **slowly / quickly** downhill.
4. Abrasion occurs as a glacier **grinds / glides** over the rock below.
5. The process of a glacier dislodging whole rocks is called **picking / plucking.**

## Did you know?

The force of the wind can cause massive erosion. The wind can whip up loose soil into huge dust storms. Dust and sand carried by the wind can wear away rock.

**Wind-eroded rock**

## Glacial erosion facts

- In high mountain regions, snow lies permanently on the ground. Even in the summer, the sun is not hot enough to melt it all.
- In some places, the weight of the accumulated snow squeezes out the air and turns the snow into ice. The ice forms a glacier that flows very slowly downward.
- A glacier dislodges rocks as it moves (this is called plucking) and carries them downhill.
- As it moves, a glacier and the rocks it contains grind the rock below, like sandpaper rubbing against wood. This is called abrasion.

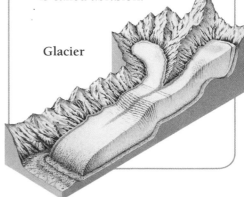

**Glacier**

# Past Climates

How do we know what the climate was like in the past? There are clues all around us, in the natural world, and in records kept by meteorologists of past centuries. Even paintings can tell us about the weather in the past. Dutch paintings from the 1600s show people skating on frozen rivers and canals during a cold period known as the Little Ice Age.

## Past climate facts

- During part of the Carboniferous period, 359 to 299 million years ago, Earth was warmer than it is today.

- Carboniferous means "coal-bearing." The fossilized remains of the vast swamps and forests that covered Earth during this era provide us with coal and other fossil fuels.

- Volcanoes can greatly affect the world's weather. Erupted ash and dust can float in the atmosphere for years, reducing the amount of sunlight reaching Earth's surface.

- The eruption of Krakatau in Indonesia in 1883 caused world temperatures to drop by 0.9°F (0.5°C).

- During the last ice age, giant creatures called woolly mammoths roamed near the edges of the ice sheets. Warmer climates and hunting by humans caused their extinction about 10,000 years ago.

## True or false?

*Using the information on this page and on page 12, check the boxes to show which facts are true and which facts are false.*

|  | TRUE | FALSE |
|---|---|---|
| 1. Times in Earth's history when ice sheets have got bigger are known as interglacials. | ☐ | ☐ |
| 2. Fossil fuels release carbon dioxide into the atmosphere when they are burned. | ☐ | ☐ |
| 3. Oil, natural gas, and coal are all fossil fuels. | ☐ | ☐ |
| 4. Volcanic eruptions can affect the weather thousands of miles from the location of the actual volcano. | ☐ | ☐ |
| 5. Warmer temperatures are often experienced after volcanic eruptions. | ☐ | ☐ |
| 6. A change in climate and being hunted by humans probably caused the extinction of the woolly mammoth. | ☐ | ☐ |

## Tree rings

*A cross section of a tree trunk can tell you about the weather in the past. Draw lines to match the following captions to the different parts of the tree.*

1. Every year, a tree grows rapidly producing **pale wood**.

2. Toward the end of the growing season, the tree's growth slows down producing **darker wood**.

3. Together the light and dark form a pattern of rings. There is **one ring** for every year of growth.

4. In years with good weather, there is good growth, so **rings are wide** in those years.

5. In years of drought, the tree does not grow as well, so the **rings are narrow**.

# Collecting Weather Data

Meteorologists collect information from a wide variety of different instruments. These range from very simple thermometers to measure temperature to rain gauges to collect and measure the amount of rainfall to highly sophisticated sensors that send back accurate data about the atmosphere far above Earth. All of this information is used to build up a picture of what the weather is doing around Earth.

## Did you know?

Weather planes drop instruments directly into hurricanes to get information about temperature, humidity, atmospheric pressure, wind speed, and wind direction. The small tube that carries the instruments is called a dropsonde. It relays information to the plane by radio transmitter.

## Information gatherers

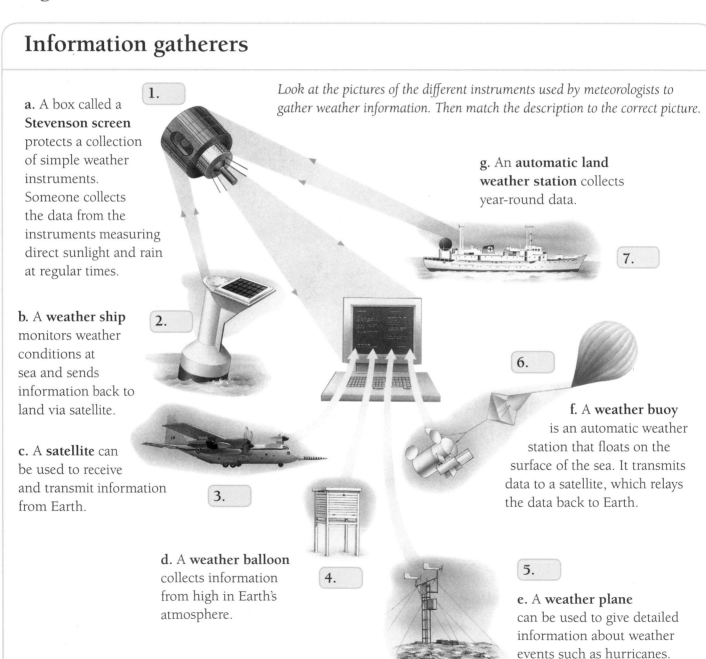

**a.** A box called a **Stevenson screen** protects a collection of simple weather instruments. Someone collects the data from the instruments measuring direct sunlight and rain at regular times.

1.

*Look at the pictures of the different instruments used by meteorologists to gather weather information. Then match the description to the correct picture.*

**g.** An **automatic land weather station** collects year-round data.

7.

**b.** A **weather ship** monitors weather conditions at sea and sends information back to land via satellite.

2.

6.

**c.** A **satellite** can be used to receive and transmit information from Earth.

3.

**f.** A **weather buoy** is an automatic weather station that floats on the surface of the sea. It transmits data to a satellite, which relays the data back to Earth.

**d.** A **weather balloon** collects information from high in Earth's atmosphere.

4.

5.

**e.** A **weather plane** can be used to give detailed information about weather events such as hurricanes.

# Meteorology quiz

*Using the information on pages 13 and 32, fill in the missing words in these sentences. Choose from:*

**Stevenson screen    radiosonde    wind speed
weather plane    geostationary**

1. Weather satellites that orbit the Earth above the same place all the time are called ............................... satellites.
2. A ........................... is the package of instruments carried by a weather balloon.
3. Meteorologists track weather balloons to get an indication of ...............................
4. A box called a ........................... is used to protect instruments from direct sunlight and rain.
5. To get detailed information about a hurricane, meteorologists often use a ...........................

# Weather watching

*This weather chart shows a typical week of weather. Using the information on the chart, see whether you can answer the questions below.*

| | General observations | Average daytime temperature | Rainfall | Wind speed |
|---|---|---|---|---|
| Monday | Sunny | 66°F | none | 5 mph |
| Tuesday | Patchy cloud | 63°C | 0.4 mm | 5 mph |
| Wednesday | Patchy cloud | 61°C | 0.8 mm | 6 mph |
| Thursday | Cloudy | 57°C | 0.9 mm | 7 mph |
| Friday | Rainy | 55°C | 1.4 mm | 12 mph |
| Saturday | Cloudy | 61°C | none | 9 mph |
| Sunday | Low cloud | 59°C | 0.5 mm | 2 mph |

1. Which was the hottest day? ...............................
2. Which day had the most rainfall? ...............................
3. Which was the windiest day? ...............................
4. Which days had no rainfall at all? ...............................
5. What was the total rainfall for the whole week? ...............................

You could try keeping a chart like this for a week. You will need a thermometer to measure the temperature, your rain gauge to measure the rainfall (see page 21), and your anemometer to measure the wind speed (see page 18). Make sure that you read your instruments at the same time each day.

# Natural forecasters

*The natural world around you gives many indications of what weather to expect. Read the following ways of forecasting wet weather using natural objects. Check the boxes to keep a record of which ones you have observed. How effective were they?*

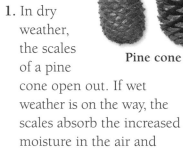

**Pine cone**

1. In dry weather, the scales of a pine cone open out. If wet weather is on the way, the scales absorb the increased moisture in the air and close up again. ☐

2. Kelp is a kind of seaweed. In dry weather, it shrivels up, but if wet weather approaches, the kelp absorbs the water vapor in the air and swells to its normal shape again. ☐

**Kelp**

3. Like kelp, wool reacts to the amount of moisture in the air. In dry weather, sheep's wool feels dry and brittle. As wet weather approaches, it becomes pliant and supple. ☐

4. The flowers of the scarlet pimpernel close up when the atmospheric pressure decreases, warning of rain on the way. ☐

**Scarlet pimpernel**

# Weather Power

Scientists believe that human activity is affecting the world's climate. Burning fossil fuels releases greenhouse gases, which are causing Earth's atmosphere to become warmer. The sun and the wind can provide alternative sources of energy. Solar and wind power are clean and renewable sources of energy because they do not create greenhouse gases, and they will never run out.

## Did you know?

Wind turbines have to be in windy places to work well. Groups of turbines, called wind farms, are often sited on hilltops or on sandbanks at sea.

## Inside a wind turbine

*Read the descriptions below of some of the features of a wind turbine. Then number the diagram 1 to 5 to match up with the descriptions.*

1. The **blades** are shaped to catch the wind.
2. The blades turn a steel **shaft**.
3. The turning movement of the shaft is converted into electricity in a small **generator**.
4. A **sensor** mounted on the wind turbine measures the wind speed and wind direction. This information is relayed to a computer, and the position of the blades is adjusted to face the wind.
5. The wind turbine is supported by a **tower** made of steel. Inside the tower are cables to carry the electricity to the grid, where it can be used in people's homes.

## Solar power facts

- Solar power stations use mirrors to gather the energy in sunlight. This energy is used to power turbines that generate electricity.
- Photovoltaic solar panels convert the sun's energy directly into electricity.
- Another type of solar energy collector uses the sun's energy to heat water in pipes for use in homes.
- Hot deserts are good places for solar power plants because they have almost unlimited sunshine during the day.

## Solar power quiz

*Fill in the missing words about solar power. Use the information on this page to help you. Choose from:*

**greenhouse gases     photovoltaic
renewable     deserts     water     mirrors**

1. Energy from the sun is a ................................. source because it will never run out.
2. Electricity produced by solar power is clean because it does not create any ......................................................
3. The sun's energy is converted directly into electricity by ................................................ solar panels.
4. The clear, cloudless skies in ................................. make these places very good locations for solar power stations.
5. Solar energy collectors are used to heat ................................
6. In solar power stations ..................... are used to gather the sun's energy.

# Pollution and Weather

Earth's atmosphere has always been affected by natural pollution, such as ash and dust from volcanic eruptions or smoke from wildfires. But pollution from human activity has increased dramatically in the last 200 years. Smoke and fumes from industry, and emissions from road vehicles and planes, now affect the atmosphere in even the remotest parts of our planet.

## Pollution facts

- Pollution can affect rain. Acid rain occurs when pollutants from industrial areas and cars interact with sunlight and water vapor. Acid rain can damage trees and crops thousands of miles from the source of the pollution.

- Cities such as New Delhi and Mexico City often suffer from photochemical smog. This occurs when pollution from cars and other vehicles reacts in the strong sunlight, creating a brown haze.

- Smoke from coal-burning fires is particularly dangerous, because it contains both greenhouse gases and particles of soot. This mixture can cause serious illnesses, as well as acid rain and smog.

- Forest fires release greenhouse gases into the atmosphere, as well as particles of soot and ash. This can result in a dramatic increase in health problems for the local population.

## True or false?

*Using the information on this page and page 12 to help you, check the boxes to show which facts are true and which are false.*

**Power stations emit greenhouse gases into the atmosphere.**

|  | TRUE | FALSE |
|---|---|---|
| 1. Methane is a greenhouse gas. | ☐ | ☐ |
| 2. Ozone helps absorb rays from the sun that can cause skin cancer. | ☐ | ☐ |
| 3. Acid rain helps plants grow. | ☐ | ☐ |
| 4. The ozone hole has been getting bigger since 1990. | ☐ | ☐ |
| 5. Cities with sunny climates and lots of cars tend to experience photochemical smogs. | ☐ | ☐ |
| 6. Soot particles from coal-burning fires can cause serious health problems. | ☐ | ☐ |

## Acid rain

*Look closely at the diagram on the right, then complete each of these sentences using the information on this page to help you.*

1. Acid rain is the result of pollution released from ........................ and .........................
2. The pollutants react with ..................... and ............................. in the atmosphere.
3. When rain falls, it is more .......... than normal.
4. Acid rain causes the soil to lose its ............... This makes trees grow more slowly, or stop growing altogether.

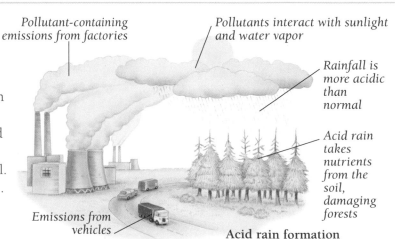

*Pollutant-containing emissions from factories*

*Pollutants interact with sunlight and water vapor*

*Rainfall is more acidic than normal*

*Acid rain takes nutrients from the soil, damaging forests*

*Emissions from vehicles*

**Acid rain formation**

# The Environment

We rely on the weather to sustain life on Earth. We need sunshine and rain for crops to grow and for animals and people to be healthy. But sometimes extremes of weather can have disastrous effects on the environment and on people. Events such as hurricanes, heat waves, blizzards, floods, and tornadoes can cause billions of dollars worth of damage and claim thousands of lives.

**Heat wave**

A heat wave that hit much of Europe in July ............... caused thousands of deaths. Record high temperatures were reached in many countries, including 101.7°F (38.7 °C) in the United Kingdom—the highest temperature there since records began.

## Weather and the environment

*This map of the world shows the locations of some weather-related disasters over the past 40 years. Fill in the missing words, using information on the chart at the back of the book to help you.*

**Ice storm**

An ice storm that caused roughly $5 billion worth of damage hit eastern Canada in ...............................19....... This ice storm also affected parts of northeastern United States. The storm brought down power lines across the region, forcing millions of people to survive without electricity in the winter cold.

North America

Europe

Atlantic Ocean

Pacific Ocean

South America

**Hurricane**

Hurricane ........................................... hit Florida, Louisiana, Mississippi, and Alabama in August 2005. It was one of the most destructive hurricanes ever to hit the United States, and it flooded 80 percent of the city of New Orleans in Louisiana.

**Avalanche**

When snow becomes unstable on a slope, it can suddenly slide down in an avalanche. Some avalanches are big enough to bury whole villages. This is what happened in Austria in 1999, when the village of Galtür was engulfed by a huge avalanche.

### Drought

A famine that killed more than 1 million people in ........................, Africa, in 1984–1985 was caused by drought and civil war. When crops failed because of the drought, rebels prevented food from reaching people in the areas they controlled.

Asia

Indian Ocean

Australia

## Extreme weather quiz

*Circle the correct words to complete each statement.*
*Use the information on page 11 to help you.*

1. Hurricanes develop when **warm, moist / cool, dry** air rises off the surface of the sea.
2. Hurricanes need a sea temperature of **less than / more than** 80°F (27°C) to develop.
3. In the Indian Ocean, hurricanes are known as **tropical cyclones / typhoons**.
4. In ice storms, the weight of the ice **can / cannot** break tree branches.
5. Heat waves are often caused by **stationary / blocking** highs, which are areas of atmospheric pressure that get stuck.
6. Lack of rainfall can result in **floods / drought**.

### Floods

In July 2005, floods hit the city of ................. in India. The rain that caused the floods was brought by the southwest monsoon. The monsoon rains were so heavy that year that the city received half of its annual average rainfall in just 24 hours. In some places, the water rose to levels that were higher than people's heads.

### Mudslides

Heavy rain can set off mudslides, when hillsides turn into fast-moving rivers of mud and debris. In 2017, a tropical storm set off a devastating mudslide and floods that buried or swept away whole villages in ........................, killing more than 200 people.

## Did you know?

In very hot weather, heatstroke can be a risk. This happens when a person's temperature rises dangerously high—usually above 105°F (40.6°C). It is vital to cool the victim down in order to lower his or her temperature.

### Bushfires

From September 2019 to March 2020, a series of fires in southeastern Australia burned about 72,000 sq miles (186,000 sq km) of bushland. The fires destroyed 5,900 buildings and killed at least 34 people.

# Weather in the Atmosphere

Check or number the boxes to answer each question. Check your answers on page 46.

**1** In which layer of the Earth's atmosphere does the world's weather occur?

- ☐ **a.** Stratosphere
- ☐ **b.** Thermosphere
- ☐ **c.** Troposphere
- ☐ **d.** Mesosphere

**2** Number these steps 1 to 4 to show how a cloud is formed.

- ☐ **a.** The tiny droplets in the air form a cloud.
- ☐ **b.** A warm patch of ground sends up a bubble of hot air.
- ☐ **c.** The ground heats up and warms the air above it.
- ☐ **d.** As the warm air rises, the water vapor begins to cool and condense.

**3** Check the three low-level clouds in this list.

- ☐ **a.** Cumulus
- ☐ **b.** Stratus
- ☐ **c.** Nimbostratus
- ☐ **d.** Cumulonimbus

**4** Which of these is *not* a high-level cloud?

- ☐ **a.** Cirrus
- ☐ **b.** Altocumulus
- ☐ **c.** Cirrocumulus
- ☐ **d.** Cirrostratus

**5** Why do you often see lightning before you hear thunder?

- ☐ **a.** Because they happen in different places.
- ☐ **b.** Because sound travels faster than light.
- ☐ **c.** Because your eyes are more sensitive than your ears.
- ☐ **d.** Because light travels faster than sound.

**6** What is the fog called that is caused by warm, moist air moving over cold land or water?

- ☐ **a.** Advection fog
- ☐ **b.** Smog
- ☐ **c.** Radiation fog
- ☐ **d.** Frost

**7** Which of these does *not* describe a type of frost?

- ☐ **a.** Rime
- ☐ **b.** Fern
- ☐ **c.** Leaf
- ☐ **d.** Hoar

**8** What are the two main causes of acid rain?

- ☐ **a.** Industrial pollution
- ☐ **b.** Volcanic eruptions
- ☐ **c.** Emissions from vehicles
- ☐ **d.** Forest fires

**9** Which of the following are greenhouse gases?

- ☐ **a.** Water vapor
- ☐ **b.** Oxygen
- ☐ **c.** Methane
- ☐ **d.** Carbon dioxide

**10** Where is the hole in the ozone layer located?

- ☐ **a.** Above the equator
- ☐ **b.** Above the North Pole
- ☐ **c.** Above the United States
- ☐ **d.** Above Antarctica

# Sun and Earth

Check or number the boxes to answer each question. Check your answers on page 46.

**1** Roughly how much of the sun's heat energy reaches the surface of our planet?

- [ ] **a.** 20 percent
- [ ] **b.** 16 percent
- [ ] **c.** 50 percent
- [ ] **d.** 4 percent

**2** Which regions of Earth receive the most heat energy from the sun?

- [ ] **a.** The poles
- [ ] **b.** The tropics
- [ ] **c.** The subtropics
- [ ] **d.** The temperate zones

**3** Which of these has the highest albedo?

- [ ] **a.** Snow
- [ ] **b.** Grass
- [ ] **c.** Wood
- [ ] **d.** Tarmac

**4** When is the longest day of the year?

- [ ] **a.** Fall
- [ ] **b.** Winter
- [ ] **c.** Summer
- [ ] **d.** Spring

**5** What are the seasons when the North Pole is tilted away from the sun?

- [ ] **a.** Summer in the northern hemisphere
- [ ] **b.** Winter in the southern hemisphere
- [ ] **c.** Winter in the northern hemisphere
- [ ] **d.** Summer in the southern hemisphere

**6** Which of these is *not* a characteristic of spring?

- [ ] **a.** Gradually rising temperatures
- [ ] **b.** Animals going into hibernation
- [ ] **c.** Days getting longer
- [ ] **d.** Plant growth

**7** How many seasons are there in many tropical regions?

- [ ] **a.** Four seasons
- [ ] **b.** Two—a wet and a dry season
- [ ] **c.** No seasons
- [ ] **d.** Three seasons

**8** Number these descriptions of the seasons 1 to 4 to put them in the correct order, starting with winter.

- [ ] **a.** Temperatures fall, and rainfall often increases.
- [ ] **b.** Temperatures rise, and the days get longer.
- [ ] **c.** Temperatures are usually high, and the days are long.
- [ ] **d.** Temperatures are low, with rain or snow, and the days are short.

**9** How many colors are there in a rainbow?

- [ ] **a.** 7
- [ ] **b.** 5
- [ ] **c.** 9
- [ ] **d.** 6

**10** What are the three main advantages of solar power?

- [ ] **a.** It does not create greenhouse gases.
- [ ] **b.** It works in cloudy weather.
- [ ] **c.** It will never run out.
- [ ] **d.** It is an alternative to burning fossil fuels.

# Air and Ocean Currents

Check or number the boxes to answer each question. Check your answers on page 46.

**1** What are two characteristics of air when it is warmed?

☐ **a.** It becomes more dense.
☐ **b.** It starts to rise.
☐ **c.** It becomes less dense.
☐ **d.** It starts to sink.

**2** Which of these words does *not* describe a type of wind?

☐ **a.** Katabatic
☐ **b.** Trade
☐ **c.** Cumulus
☐ **d.** Prevailing

**3** What is the cause of the deflection of winds called the Coriolis effect?

☐ **a.** Temperature differences
☐ **b.** Differences in atmospheric pressure
☐ **c.** Tall mountains
☐ **d.** Earth's spinning motion

**4** Which two are alternative names for a hurricane?

☐ **a.** A tropical cyclone
☐ **b.** A tornado
☐ **c.** A typhoon
☐ **d.** A gustnado

**5** What are two of the typical effects of an El Niño event?

☐ **a.** Less rainfall in Australia
☐ **b.** More rainfall in Australia
☐ **c.** More rainfall in South America
☐ **d.** Less rainfall in South America

**6** Which of these are ocean currents?

☐ **a.** Mistral
☐ **b.** Humboldt
☐ **c.** Gulf Stream
☐ **d.** Benguela

**7** Number these events 1 to 4 to describe the formation of a hurricane.

☐ **a.** Winds starts to blow in a circular pattern.
☐ **b.** Gigantic cumulonimbus clouds build up.
☐ **c.** Air rushes into the area of low atmospheric pressure just above the surface of the water.
☐ **d.** Huge amounts of water evaporate off the surface of the warm sea.

**8** If the temperature outside is 14°F and the wind chill temperature is 9°F, what is the actual temperature of the air?

☐ **a.** 9°F
☐ **b.** 14°F
☐ **c.** 27°F
☐ **d.** −9°F

**9** What is a sea breeze?

☐ **a.** A wind that blows across the open sea
☐ **b.** A wind that blows from land to sea
☐ **c.** A wind that blows from sea to land

**10** What is the Beaufort scale used to describe?

☐ **a.** The strength of the wind
☐ **b.** The strength of the sun
☐ **c.** Atmospheric pressure
☐ **d.** The strength of a current

# Rain, Hail, and Snow

Check or number the boxes to answer each question. Check your answers on page 46.

**1** Which of these is *not* precipitation?

- ☐ a. Rain
- ☐ b. Hail
- ☐ c. Snow
- ☐ d. Humidity
- ☐ e. Sleet

**2** What size raindrops are classed as drizzle?

- ☐ a. More than 0.02 in (0.5 mm) across
- ☐ b. Less than 0.02 in (0.5 mm) across
- ☐ c. Less than 0.2 in (5 mm) across

**3** How do meteorologists define heavy rain?

- ☐ a. More than 0.3 in (7.5 mm) in an hour
- ☐ b. More than 0.02 in (0.5 mm) in an hour
- ☐ c. More than 0.08 in (2 mm) in an hour

**4** What are three possible consequences of too little rain?

- ☐ a. Floods
- ☐ b. Drought
- ☐ c. Famine
- ☐ d. Wildfires

**5** What is a blizzard?

- ☐ a. A rainstorm
- ☐ b. A snowstorm with high winds
- ☐ c. A strong wind
- ☐ d. A snowfall

**6** Number these statements 1 to 4 to describe the life cycle of a hailstone.

- ☐ a. The hail embryo becomes covered in layers of freezing water and ice.
- ☐ b. Powerful air currents carry the hail embryo up and down.
- ☐ c. A hailstone starts life as a hail embryo.
- ☐ d. The hail embryo becomes heavy enough to drop to earth as a hailstone.

**7** What is sleet?

- ☐ a. Cold rain
- ☐ b. Heavy rain
- ☐ c. A mixture of rain and wet snow
- ☐ d. Thick snow

**8** Number these statements 1 to 4 to describe the rain shadow effect.

- ☐ a. Moist, warm air is forced upward when it meets a mountain range.
- ☐ b. Dry air flows across the mountains to the leeward side.
- ☐ c. Rain falls from the clouds on the windward side of the mountain.
- ☐ d. As the air rises, it cools and condenses, forming clouds.

**9** Which two of these events can be caused by heavy rainfall?

- ☐ a. Mudslides
- ☐ b. Avalanches
- ☐ c. Floods
- ☐ d. Ice storms

**10** From which direction does the wet Asian monsoon wind blow?

- ☐ a. Northeast
- ☐ b. Southwest
- ☐ c. Southeast
- ☐ d. Northwest

# Climate and Climate Change

Check or number the boxes to answer each question. Check your answers on page 46.

**1** Which climate is hot and wet all year round?

- [ ] **a.** Subtropical
- [ ] **b.** Mediterranean
- [ ] **c.** Tropical monsoon
- [ ] **d.** Tropical

**2** Which climate has less than 10in (250mm) rainfall per year?

- [ ] **a.** Desert
- [ ] **b.** Continental
- [ ] **c.** Semiarid
- [ ] **d.** Temperate

**3** Select the three typical features of a Mediterranean climate.

- [ ] **a.** Chaparral vegetation
- [ ] **b.** High rainfall in winters
- [ ] **c.** Hot summers
- [ ] **d.** Extremely cold winters

**4** Which bird holds the record for the longest distance migration?

- [ ] **a.** Sparrow
- [ ] **b.** Swallow
- [ ] **c.** Arctic tern
- [ ] **d.** Albatross

**5** Which of the following have adaptations that allow them to survive in cold climates?

- [ ] **a.** Penguin
- [ ] **b.** Camel
- [ ] **c.** Snow leopard
- [ ] **d.** Coniferous tree

**6** Roughly when did the last Ice Age end?

- [ ] **a.** 1 million years ago
- [ ] **b.** 100,000 years ago
- [ ] **c.** 1,000 years ago
- [ ] **d.** 11,500 years ago

**7** Which is *not* a possible effect of global warming?

- [ ] **a.** Raised sea levels
- [ ] **b.** More extreme weather
- [ ] **c.** Lowered sea levels
- [ ] **d.** Melting ice sheets

**8** Number these descriptions 1 to 4 in the order you might experience them as you climbed up a mountain in the Himalayas.

- [ ] **a.** Permanent ice and snow cover
- [ ] **b.** The tree line
- [ ] **c.** Subtropical forests
- [ ] **d.** High alpine grasslands

**9** What is a maritime climate?

- [ ] **a.** A warm climate
- [ ] **b.** A climate that is affected by the sea
- [ ] **c.** A wet climate
- [ ] **d.** A mountain climate

**10** Which place on Earth holds the record for the driest climate?

- [ ] **a.** Sahara, North Africa
- [ ] **b.** Atacama Desert, Chile
- [ ] **c.** Great Sandy Desert, Australia
- [ ] **d.** Thar Desert, Pakistan/India

# Weather Forecasting

Check or number the boxes to answer each question. Check your answers on page 46.

**1** What is the term for a weather scientist?

- ☐ **a.** Zoologist
- ☐ **b.** Pharmacologist
- ☐ **c.** Meteorologist
- ☐ **d.** Hydrologist

**2** At roughly what height do geostationary satellites orbit Earth?

- ☐ **a.** 2,240 miles (3,600 km)
- ☐ **b.** 6,200 miles (10,000 km)
- ☐ **c.** 24,900 miles (40,000 km)
- ☐ **d.** 22,400 miles (36,000 km)

**3** What is a radiosonde?

- ☐ **a.** An instrument in a weather satellite
- ☐ **b.** An instrument attached to a weather balloon
- ☐ **c.** An instrument dropped by a weather plane

**4** Number these steps 1 to 4 to describe a warm front.

- ☐ **a.** Denser, cooler air falls
- ☐ **b.** Warm air rises.
- ☐ **c.** Clouds often bring rain
- ☐ **d.** Warm air condenses to form clouds

**5** Which air mass is defined as warm and moist over oceans?

- ☐ **a.** Tropical continental
- ☐ **b.** Polar continental
- ☐ **c.** Polar maritime
- ☐ **d.** Tropical maritime

**6** Which of these instruments is *not* used to collect data about the weather?

- ☐ **a.** Wind vane
- ☐ **b.** Thermometer
- ☐ **c.** Radiator
- ☐ **d.** Rain gauge

**7** How is weather data collected from the seas and oceans?

- ☐ **a.** By weather balloon
- ☐ **b.** By weather ship
- ☐ **c.** Using a Stevenson screen
- ☐ **d.** By weather buoy

**8** What does an anemometer measure?

- ☐ **a.** Wind speed
- ☐ **b.** Amount of rain
- ☐ **c.** Amount of sunlight
- ☐ **d.** Wind direction

**9** Which of these could help you predict the weather?

- ☐ **a.** A stone
- ☐ **b.** A pine cone
- ☐ **c.** A piece of kelp
- ☐ **d.** A scarlet pimpernel

**10** What are the fastest winds measured in a hurricane?

- ☐ **a.** Up to 310 mph (500 km/h)
- ☐ **b.** Up to 185 mph (300 km/h)
- ☐ **c.** Up to 124 mph (200 km/h)
- ☐ **d.** Up to 62 mph (100 km/h)

# Activity Answers

Once you have completed each page of activities, check your answers below.

## Page 14
### Which climate?
2 Very cold winter; short, cool summer
3 Polar
4 Temperate
5 Hot summers; cold winters
6 Semiarid
7 Subtropical
8 Hot and wet all year round
9 Desert

## Page 15
### Climate adaptations
1 Camel
2 Penguin
3 Snow leopard
4 Rain forest tree
5 Coniferous tree
6 Cactus

### Homes and climate
1 mud
2 igloos
3 yurts
4 roofs

## Page 16
### See for yourself
Number 2 is bigger because the flashlight beam is striking the paper at an angle, so the light is more spread out. When the flashlight beam is directly overhead, the light is brighter and more concentrated.

### Sun test
1 half
2 albedo
3 more
4 toward
5 seven
6 reddish-orange

## Page 17
### Naming currents

### El Niño

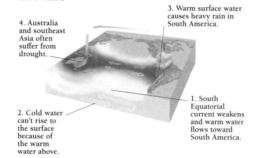

4. Australia and southeast Asia often suffer from drought.

3. Warm surface water causes heavy rain in South America.

2. Cold water can't rise to the surface because of the warm water above.

1. South Equatorial current weakens and warm water flows toward South America.

## Page 19
### What is wind chill?
1 32°F
2 −2°F
3 5°F
4 9 mph

### Twister puzzle
1 Wall cloud
2 Funnel
3 Devastation

## Page 20
### Masses of air

## Warm and cold fronts
### Warm front
1 Clouds
2 Denser, cooler air
3 Warmer air
4 Rain

### Cold front
1 Storm clouds
2 Dense, cold air
3 Steep slope
4 Warmer air

## Page 21
### True or false?
1 False—winds blow from areas of high to areas of low pressure
2 True
3 False—it comes from the Indian Ocean
4 True
5 False—it creates low pressure

## Page 23
### Cloud name activity
1 Cirrus
2 Nimbostratus
3 Stratus
4 Cumulonimbus

### Match the sky

## Page 24
### How a hurricane works

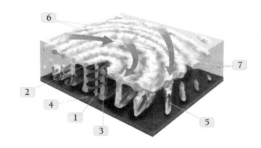

**Page 25**
**True or false?**
1 False—cumulonimbus clouds are thunderclouds
2 True
3 False—positively charged particles pile up at the top of the cloud
4 True
5 True

**What is lightning?**
1 leader stroke
2 return stroke
3 shock wave
4 several flashes

**Page 26**
**Making hail**

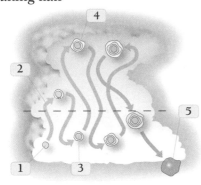

**Snow test**
1 ice crystals
2 six / different
3 snowdrift
4 dry
5 very

**Page 27**
**True or false?**
1 False—fog is thicker than mist
2 True
3 False— they happen when water vapor condenses
4 False—it happens on clear, calm nights
5 True
6 True

**Frost puzzle**
1 b  2 c  3 a

**Page 28**
**Rain shadow puzzle**

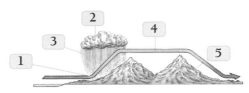

**Mountain zones**
The lammergeier lives among the **mountain** peaks ...
High **alpine** grasslands ...
The coniferous forests ... are home to ... the **red panda**
The snow leopard ... can survive ... at high **altitude**
The **tree line**—the point where the climate becomes too cold for trees to survive ...
At the base of the Himalayas ... **deciduous** forests ...

**Page 29**
**Coastal weather test**
1 sea
2 advection
3 wet
4 mild / warm
4 grinds
5 plucking

**Land and sea breezes**
1 land / sea
2 cool
3 loses heat
4 warm

**Page 30**
**Water to ice**
As the water freezes, it expands, widening the cracks in the rocks.

**Erosion quiz**
1 some of
2 ice
3 slowly

**Page 31**
**True or false?**
1 False—ice ages
2 True
3 True
4 True
5 False—levels of ash and dust in the atmosphere can increase, blocking the sun's rays and reducing temperatures worldwide
6 True

**Tree rings**

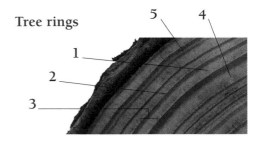

**Page 32**
**Information gatherers**
1 c  2 f  3 e  4 a  5 g  6 d  7 b

**Page 33**
**Meteorology quiz**
1 geostationary
2 radiosonde
3 wind speed
4 Stevenson screen
5 weather plane

**Weather watching**
1 Monday
2 Friday
3 Friday
4 Monday and Saturday
5 4 mm

**Page 34**
**Inside a wind turbine**

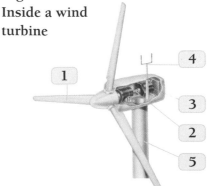

## Answers

### Page 34
**Solar power quiz**
1 renewable
2 greenhouse gases
3 photovoltaic
4 deserts
5 water
6 mirrors

### Page 35
**True or false?**
1 True
2 True
3 False—it takes nutrients from the soil, affecting plant growth

4 False—the ozone hole has got smaller
5 True
6 True

**Acid rain**
1 vehicles / factories
2 sunlight / water vapor
3 acidic
4 nutrients

### Pages 36–37
**Weather and the environment**
**Heat wave**—2019
**Drought**—Ethiopia

**Floods**—Mumbai
**Hurricane**—Katrina
**Ice storm**—January 1998
**Mudslides**—the Philippines

### Page 37
**Extreme weather quiz**
1 warm, moist
2 more than
3 tropical cyclones
4 can
5 blocking
6 drought

# Quick Quiz Answers
Once you have completed each page of quiz questions, check your answers below.

### Page 38
**Weather in the Atmosphere**
1 c 2 c 1, b 2, d 3, a 4 3 a, b, d 4 b
5 d 6 a 7 c 8 a, c 9 a, c, d 10 d

### Page 39
**Sun and Earth**
1 c 2 b 3 a 4 c 5 c, d 6 b 7 b, c
8 d 1, b 2, c 3, a 4 9 a 10 a, c, d

### Page 40
**Air and Ocean Currents**
1 b, c 2 c 3 d 4 a, c 5 a, c 6 b, c, d

7 d 1, b 2, c 3, a 4 8 b 9 c 10 a

### Page 41
**Rain, Hail, and Snow**
1 d 2 b 3 a 4 b, c, d 5 b 6 c 1,
b 2, a 3, d 4 7 c 8 a 1, d 2, c 3, b 4
9 a, c 10 b

### Page 42
**Climate and Climate Change**
1 d 2 a 3 a, b, c 4 c 5 a, c, d 6 d
7 c 8 c 1, b 2, d 3, a 4 9 b 10 b

### Page 43
**Weather Forecasting**
1 c 2 d 3 b 4 b 1, a 2, d 3, c 4 5 d
6 c 7 b, d 8 a 9 b, c, d 10 b

---

# Acknowledgments

**The publisher would like to thank the following:**

Stewart J Wild and Julie Ferris for proof-reading, Robert Dinwiddie for 2020 consultant review, and Harish Aggarwal and Priyanka Sharma for the jacket.

The publisher would like to thank the following for their kind permission to reproduce their photographs:

(Key: a-above; b-below/bottom; c-center; f-far; l-left; r-right; t-top)

NASA: 6 (bc). 13 Finley Holiday Films (bl). 24 Finley Holiday Films (cra). DK Images:

29 Dan Bannister (ca). 41 Rough Guides (br).

All other images © Dorling Kindersley For further information see: www.dkimages.com

# CLIMATE ZONES

| REGION | TROPICAL | TROPICAL MONSOON | TROPICAL WET/DRY |
|---|---|---|---|
| LOCATIONS | AMAZON BASIN, SOUTH AMERICA; MALAYSIA, INDONESIA | INDIA, BANGLADESH, MYANMAR | CENTRAL AFRICA, BRAZIL, VENEZUELA |
| SEASONS | NO DRY SEASON | SHORT DRY SEASON | DISTINCT WET AND DRY SEASONS |
| FEATURES | HOT AND WET ALL YEAR ROUND | SEASONAL RAINFALL BROUGHT BY MONSOON | COOLER DURING THE DRY SEASON |
| VEGETATION | RAIN FOREST | MONSOON FOREST | SAVANNA |

| REGION | DESERT | SEMIARID | SUBTROPICAL |
|---|---|---|---|
| LOCATIONS | NORTH AFRICA, MEXICO, CENTRAL AUSTRALIA | EURASIAN STEPPE; WESTERN UNITED STATES | SOUTHEASTERN UNITED STATES, EASTERN AUSTRALIA |
| SEASONS | DRY AND HOT ALL YEAR ROUND | DRY HOT SUMMERS; COLD WINTERS | HOT SUMMERS; MILD WINTERS |
| FEATURES | LESS THAN 10 IN (250 MM) RAINFALL PER YEAR | MORE RAINFALL THAN DESERT CLIMATES | HIGH HUMIDITY; SUMMER STORMS |
| VEGETATION | CACTI | SHORT GRASSLAND | EVERGREEN FOREST |

| REGION | MEDITERRANEAN | TEMPERATE | CONTINENTAL |
|---|---|---|---|
| LOCATIONS | CALIFORNIA; BORDERS OF THE MEDITERRANEAN SEA | WESTERN EUROPE; WESTERN NORTH AMERICA | MIDWESTERN UNITED STATES |
| SEASONS | HOT SUMMERS; COLD WINTERS | WARM SUMMERS; MILD WINTERS | HOT SUMMERS; COLD WINTERS |
| FEATURES | LOW RAINFALL IN SUMMER; HIGH IN WINTER | HIGH RAINFALL THROUGHOUT THE YEAR | WINTER SNOW COVER |
| VEGETATION | CHAPARRAL | DECIDUOUS FOREST | GRASSLAND AND FOREST |

| REGION | TAIGA | TUNDRA | POLAR |
|---|---|---|---|
| LOCATIONS | NORTHERN CANADA; ALASKA; EURASIA | ARCTIC COASTAL AREAS | ARCTIC; ANTARCTIC |
| SEASONS | VERY COLD WINTER; SHORT, COOL SUMMER | COLD ALL YEAR ROUND | EXTREME COLD YEAR ROUND |
| FEATURES | WINTER SNOW COVER; HUMID IN SUMMER | PERMANENTLY FROZEN GROUND | ICE AND SNOW |
| VEGETATION | CONIFEROUS FOREST | LOW SHRUBS, LICHEN, MOSS | NONE |

## WEATHER EXTREMES

| RECORD | LOWEST RECORDED TEMPERATURE | HIGHEST RECORDED TEMPERATURE | WETTEST PLACE |
|---|---|---|---|
| STATISTICS | TEMPERATURE −128.6°F (−89.2°C) | TEMPERATURE 134.1°F (56.7°C) | ANNUAL 467.5 IN (11,872 MM) RAINFALL PER YEAR |
| LOCATION | VOSTOK | DEATH VALLEY, CALIFORNIA | MAWSYNRAM, INDIA |
| CONTINENT | ANTARCTICA | NORTH AMERICA | ASIA |
| DATE | JULY 21, 1983 | JULY 10, 1913 | AVERAGE OVER 38 YEARS |

| RECORD | DRIEST PLACE | FASTEST WIND | BIGGEST HAILSTONE |
|---|---|---|---|
| STATISTICS | 0.6 IN (15 MM) OF RAIN ANNUALLY | TORNADO SPEED 318 MILES (512 KM) PER HOUR | 8 IN (20 CM) IN DIAMETER; 18.6 IN (47.3 CM) IN CIRCUMFERENCE |
| LOCATION | ATACAMA DESERT, CHILE | OKLAHOMA CITY, OKLAHOMA | VIVIAN, SOUTH DAKOTA |
| CONTINENT | SOUTH AMERICA | NORTH AMERICA | NORTH AMERICA |
| DATE | AVERAGE MORE THAN 60 YEARS | MAY 3, 1999 | JULY 23, 2010 |

## WEATHER DISASTERS

| EVENT | HURRICANE KATRINA | HEAT WAVE | ICE STORM |
|---|---|---|---|
| DATE | AUGUST 2005 | JULY 2019 | JANUARY 1998 |
| LOCATION | FLORIDA, LOUISIANA, MISSISSIPPI, ALABAMA | WESTERN EUROPE | CANADA AND NORTHEASTERN US |
| CONTINENT | NORTH AMERICA | EUROPE | NORTH AMERICA |
| DAMAGE | KILLED MORE THAN 1,800 PEOPLE | KILLED SEVERAL THOUSAND PEOPLE | CAUSED $5 BILLION WORTH OF DAMAGE |

| EVENT | FLOODS | DROUGHT | MUDSLIDE |
|---|---|---|---|
| DATE | JULY 2005 | 1984–1985 | 2017 |
| LOCATION | MUMBAI, INDIA | ETHIOPIA | THE PHILIPPINES |
| CONTINENT | ASIA | AFRICA | ASIA |
| DAMAGE | KILLED MORE THAN 1,000 PEOPLE | 1 MILLION PEOPLE DIED | KILLED MORE THAN 200 PEOPLE |